Kindergarten Simplified

Kindergarten Simplified

✦

A No-Nonsense Guide for Busy Parents

Mary Lou Podlasiak

iUniverse, Inc.
New York   Bloomington

Kindergarten Simplified
A No-Nonsense Guide for Busy Parents

iUniverse books may be ordered through booksellers or by contacting:

iUniverse
1663 Liberty Drive
Bloomington, IN 47403
www.iuniverse.com
1-800-Authors (1-800-288-4677)

ISBN: 978-0-595-52868-4 (pbk)
ISBN: 978-0-595-62923-7 (ebk)

Printed in the United States of America

Also by Mary Lou Podlasiak

Rules for Roommates: The Ultimate Guide to Reclaiming Your Space and Your Sanity

It's Only a Game…Unless You're Married to the Coach

Credits

Cover photo and design by Jennifer Croucher

Children (left to right): Kristin Roessler, Jonah Croucher, Elle Schafer, & Kaylin Roessler.

Edited by Katie N. Kelly

I owe an incredible debt of gratitude to an endless parade of people who have contributed to this project, and I sorely regret that I didn't keep track of every last one of them. Even though singling out specific individuals is a risky thing to do, I still feel the need to thank those who played the biggest part in never letting me forget that I had a book to finish.

Thanks to Jennifer Croucher for your creative input, and for allowing me unlimited access to Jonah, my favorite "laboratory mouse." To Dona McConnell, the patron saint of writers, for helping me overcome my referencing deficiencies and overall paranoia. To Janet Crum, Darlene Bettinger, and Debbie Hansis, whom I consider to be the epitome of effective kindergarten teachers, for being much kinder and more patient with me than I ever deserved. To Katie Kelly, for your aggressive attempt at preventing me from embarrassing myself, (and I apologize for anything I added after you were finished!). To Diana Beaty, also a seasoned counselor, for enthusiastically sharing your extensive knowledge about elementary students. To Ruth Nau and Lindsey McConnell, for your expert opinions on medical issues. To Wendy Craycraft, for trusting me enough to gleefully hand over a copy of your entire graduate research project, (*The Relationship between Age, Kindergarten Enrollment, and Academic Achievement*). And as always, to my husband, Plaz, for intuitively knowing when to drag me away from my computer and back out into the real world.

To Connie McConnell...

Few people are lucky enough to work with a brilliant colleague who can always be trusted to give you an honest opinion, who isn't the least bit interested in advertising your mistakes, and who would never think of smirking while you're limping through the learning phase of a new career. It's also been nice to have had someone willing to clue me in on the realities of what it's really like to work in an elementary school—information far more valuable than those "theoretical educational models" that researchers and college professors dream up.

I don't know how many people saw the pizza-sauce handprint on my rump during one of my first days on the job, but Connie was the only one with the guts to break it to me. It was then that she gave me my first pearl of wisdom: *Only an idiot would wear dry-clean only clothes to school.* Soon after, she educated me on the health risks of eating leftover party treats—right after she caught me devouring a cupcake that had been re-iced with a germy finger. Just about the time I had begun to feel pretty cavalier about my knowledge of the nuances of working with elementary students, she cautioned me to be highly suspicious of anyone headed to the nurse's office—once again, too late, because I'd just bear-hugged a stream of students lining up for a lice check.

One of my greatest aspirations is to be as competent, driven, and loved as she continues to be in spite of having faced a never-ending parade of needy children for nearly three decades. I vow to the end to keep trying to emulate her skill at outfoxing persistently difficult students.

"You will always be your child's favorite toy."

~Vicki Lansky, Author

Contents

Preface

First of all, I'd like to thank you on behalf of your child for taking an interest in learning how to foster the academic, physical, and social development needed for success in school. On the other hand, I hope you haven't picked up this book with the intention of doing absolutely everything I say, and doing it perfectly. I would hate to think I've only added to the relentless pressure of the media and well-meaning acquaintances taunting you to do this and do that or you'll surely bungle your reputation as a parent. My aim is to enlighten you about the educational process to help you become more effective without feeling like you have to go at it full-throttle all the time. Hopefully you'll feel confident that you're doing enough so you'll still have time to enjoy the most formative year of your child's formal education.

Be forewarned that if you are ramped up and ready to drill every last bit of information you can get into that little head, then you're going to end up creating one miserable little creature. Building optimum skills should be an enjoyable experience, not an endless, stress-filled showdown to achieve. Becoming a more effective parent doesn't take much more time than you would normally spend together, and it doesn't take much money. Primarily, it involves simple adjustments in the way you connect verbally and emotionally, adding some structure and physical activity to your day, and paying more attention to the wondrous and infinite possibilities the world has to offer.

Please keep in mind that every school is unique in some way, whether it differs in day-to-day procedures, rules, or adopted teaching methods, so you should not consider the information I've provided as gospel. When faced with serious concerns, make sure you consult with school officials and/or professionals in your community.

Whatever you do, don't miss out on the magic and fun of your child beginning this wonderful adventure. This could be the perfect time for you to make some refreshing changes in your life as well by recapturing that sense of curiosity, playfulness, and enthusiasm for new ideas and experiences.

Lastly, I want to encourage you to search for children's books that may address some of the stumbling blocks you'll encounter along the way. I've suggested some of my favorites, but I hope you'll look for additional good stories and share them with other parents and/or your child's teacher.

(Suggested reading: *Oh, the Places You'll Go!* by Dr. Seuss.)

Every Efficient Operation Has a "Central Command Station"

Let's begin with something concrete that you can start working on right this minute to simplify the whole process of keeping it together from kindergarten throughout high school. Take a good look at the place where family members are most likely to dump things as they come in through the door. This is the area that you need to systemize so that it will work *for* you instead of against you. Even though your main focus should be on transforming this area so you'll be able to find anything and everything needed for school at a moment's notice, you will also need to create a workable setup for your entire family to keep everyone's gear separated.

You don't have to spend a fortune on organizational tools. Look at what you already have and improvise. Consider these ideas to get started creating your own functional space:

> ➤ You can place a wide bookshelf on its side, add some hooks and you'll have an inexpensive set of cubbies. You can place baskets or storage bins on top or at the bottom of each space.
> ➤ Stack up milk crates, square baskets, or other containers on their sides to create shelves for shoes, books, and the like.
> ➤ If you have an unused desk with drawers, move it into this area and place a coat rack or sturdy hall tree next to it.
> ➤ If you are lucky enough to have a closet conveniently located in this area, enhance its usability by placing hooks and shelves within reach for each family member.
> ➤ If you're fussy about decorating you may want to take a look at the entryway furniture that is becoming popular not only at upscale furniture stores, but at discount department stores as well.

This area can also be the place where you can house the information you'll need to start collecting for registration such as the names, addresses, and phone numbers of your pediatrician and/or family doctor, optometrist, dentist, and preferred hospital. Once school begins, it can serve as a buffer against the morning rush hour in your home. You can use it, for example, as a place to put the exact amount of cash needed for lunches or fees in sealable plastic sandwich bags or envelopes labeled with your child's name, amount, and its purpose. If you can't follow through with that level of organization, you can at least be sure that this will be the place where you'll put everything needed for the following day before you go to bed.

As the years pass, this designated spot will remain functional as the place where you'll easily be able to retrieve things such as yearbook receipts, permission slips for field trips, and before you know it, high school graduation announcements. For now, it can simply be the place where you know you'll be able to find this book when preparing for registration, shopping for school clothes, or trying to decide whether or not to delay enrollment for another year.

Registration Papers

(Information You Will Need and How to Get It)

I'm sorry to say that you'll be the one doing the first big homework assignment, and it will be a doozey. You will be expected to provide certain legal documents and other information that may take a little digging to find. Laws and rules vary slightly from state to state and school to school, but basically, everything is pretty much the same as described in this chapter. Just be sure you plan ahead so you won't have to scramble at the last minute to complete the required paperwork. Some schools exclude students until every last form is completed and every legal document reviewed.

Registration usually begins in the spring preceding the first day of school in order to take the guesswork out of how many students will be entering school and what their specific educational needs will be. This will allow plenty of time for you to complete the enrollment process as long as you don't procrastinate.

Social Security Card

A photocopy may or may not be accepted. Be prepared to present the original, which will be returned to you after a photocopy is made for the student's file. If you can't locate the original, visit your local Social Security office, or go online (www.socialsecurity.gov) to obtain an application for a new card.

According to the official government website, you will need to present your child's birth certificate and proof of your identify when you submit the application. A driver's license or other photo identification will suffice. If for some reason the name on the birth certificate is incorrect, you will need to have it legally changed before filing for a new card or it will also be printed incorrectly.[1]

Birth Certificate

If you do not have a government issued copy, you need to get one and keep it where you can find it. (Before you know it, it will be time to apply for a driver's permit!) You can generally obtain one by contacting the Office of Vital Statistics in the county in which your child was born. In more rural areas, you may need to contact your local health department. Either one of these offices will be able to point you in the right direction.

Many county or state websites have simple instructions for ordering a copy through the mail, so do not use any non-government sites which charge ridiculous fees for this service. You would be providing the same information, so you're better off doing it yourself.

Lastly, a child who has immigrated to the U.S., and does not have a birth certificate must be granted enrollment as long as proof can be provided that the parents reside within the school district.[2]

Proof of Legal Name

Whoever is in charge of maintaining school records will rely upon on the birth certificate for the exact spelling of a student's legal name.

<u>If the name was originally spelled incorrectly, you need to obtain a corrected certificate *before* you begin the enrollment process.</u>

Let's say your daughter's name is "Julie," but some incompetent fool recorded it as "Julei." This is a change that obviously deserves to be made without any hassle through your Office of Vital Statistics or health department, whichever maintains birth records of the county in which your child was born. The problem is, the longer you wait to make the correction, the less likely it will be done without a court order. For example, the Minnesota Department of Health only allows corrections to be made without documentation for 45 days following a birth.[3]

Another regret parents often have is being creative with spelling. Let's say you originally spelled your daughter's name "Jewelly" and have decided to change it to the more traditional spelling of "Julie." You would need to obtain an official court order to make the change by hiring an attorney to do it for you, or by filing a request yourself through your local court system. The upside of this is that you shouldn't be turned down unless your intentions appear to be fraudulent or malicious. Once the change order is signed by a judge, you can present it to have a corrected birth certificate printed.[4]

<u>If you have been referring to your child by a name that isn't on the birth certificate, and haven't gotten around to legally changing it, you need to complete the process before school begins.</u>

Starting school is scary enough without thinking that no one knows your real name. An example of a recent trend that seems to be backfiring is giving offspring hyphenated last names, such as McConnell-Epstein. Many parents are deciding that double names are not worth the hassle of learning to spell or write and rarely fit on signature lines anyway. Dropping one or the other, I'm sorry to say, must be done through a court of law as well.[5]

Another common scenario is intending to "adopt" a stepchild, but never quite getting around to doing it legally. Again, whatever is printed on the birth certificate is what will be entered in the student database and printed on all school records and documents.

Nicknames are a different story.

Most teachers do not mind using them as long as you understand that official student records, such as grade cards, will be maintained under the legal name. From the beginning, you should coach your child to answer to his or her legal name, and know the difference.

Before you know it, it will be time to fill out an application for a driver's permit and financial aid for college. Any discrepancies between the name registered with the Social Security Administration and many application forms will initiate an ugly paper chase that will delay processing.

Proof of Residency

If you know that you are not a legal resident within a school district, be truthful about it or you may end up being slapped with a tuition bill and/or charged with falsifying information. Schools that are attractive because of new facilities, academic programs, effective teachers, and student achievement do not want explosive enrollment jeopardizing what employees have worked hard to build and maintain. If the district can handle more students, they will probably accept them depending upon their "open enrollment" policies. If you are turned down and can afford it, offer to pay tuition and you'll probably be granted admission.

The downside of enrolling in a school outside of your district of residence is that you will more than likely be required to provide your own transportation. In the long run, this could become an inconvenience which may necessitate having to change schools. "Traveling" students also have a tendency to feel isolated socially. They are not purposely rejected by their peers; they just don't have as much in common with local students because their paths rarely cross outside of school.

To prove that you are a resident within the district, you may be asked to provide one or more documents bearing your name and current address. These items are typically acceptable:

> Deed or escrow papers for a home.
> Property tax receipt.
> Rental contract.
> Rental deposit receipt.
> Rent receipt.
> Utility contract and/or bill.
> Verification of voter registration.
> Motor registration.
> Driver's license.
> Current bank statement.
> Other credible pieces of mail stating your correct address and a current date.

Proof of Custody

Only a custodial parent will be permitted to enroll a child in school. If you are divorced, separated, or raising someone else's child, you will need to provide proof that you are the custodian of the child.[6] A notarized statement from the biological parent(s) or a letter from an attorney means nothing. You must provide legal documentation that has been signed by a judge such as a temporary custody order, separation agreement or final divorce decree. If you file for custody, a temporary court order placing the child in your home supersedes any previous paperwork. School officials adhere to what is expressed in the most recent documentation provided.

If you are the child's mother and have never been married to the biological father, most states automatically consider you to be the custodial parent so you may not need paperwork of any kind. The biological father would be required to provide a court document to prove otherwise.

There are, of course, some special circumstances that will immediately be taken into account. If a restraining order has been issued that includes the child's name as part of the protective custody plan, the school will adamantly honor this protection plan. If the restraining order has not yet been processed but a parent and child are being temporarily housed in a shelter due to a domestic violence incident, and authorities can authenticate the situation for school employees, then the child, or children, may be enrolled.

If you are in the military and will be deployed, contact your legal counsel for the proper paperwork to cover your caregiver while you are away.

Regardless of your situation, you will be asked to provide the non-custodial parent's full name, address, place of employment, and home and work phone numbers. If you are reluctant to pass along an estranged parent's information, just think of it as an additional safety measure. The more school employees know, the better prepared they will be for any surprise visits.

Immunization Record

There are no federal laws dictating required immunizations. State health departments decide which vaccines school-aged children should receive, but most lists are the same. Nevertheless, the requirements are constantly evolving in response to new advances in medicine; therefore, in order to receive up-to-date information you should contact your pediatrician, local health department, or your school nurse.

Your failure to comply with required immunizations may mean exclusion from school, so do not wait until the last minute to take care of business. It would also be beneficial to act as soon as possible so that the negative experience of getting shots will not be associated with going to school. Doing so will also guarantee that you will have a copy of the immunization record in time for registration.

If you forgo immunizing your child for medical, philosophical, or religious reasons, you'll need to find out what documentation you will be required to provide. You may need a statement from your clergy or health care provider, or simply your own written declaration absolving the school of any related liabilities.

(Suggested reading: *Lions Aren't Scared of Shots: A Story for Children about Visiting the Doctor* by Howard J. Bennett.)

Results of a Complete Physical Examination

This requirement varies more than any other. Even though it may not be mandatory, you might want to have one conducted for your own peace of mind. It would certainly be nice to know that there aren't any general health issues that could hinder learning.

If one is required, your health care provider will know what information should be included in the report. (For example, some impoverished areas still require screening for lead poisoning.)

(Suggested reading: *The Berenstain Bears Go to the Doctor* by Stan Berenstain and Jan Berenstain.)

Other Health Information

Health Care Providers

Be prepared to provide the names, addresses, and phone numbers of your pediatrician, family doctor, dentist, and any other health care specialists that may need to be consulted or notified in case of an emergency. Most importantly, you will be asked to designate which local hospital you prefer. You would be wise to also give your permission for your child to be transported to an appropriate facility if the school nurse or other medical personnel on the scene feel that the illness or injury is serious enough to take action before you can be contacted. If you wish, you may also choose to state the names of the facilities you would rather not patronize.

Emergency Medical Information

In addition to your list of health care providers, you will be asked to provide the names and phone numbers of people you would trust to step in and make decisions in the event that you cannot be contacted. This list should also include people willing to take responsibility and pick up your child from school in case you cannot be reached or if you simply cannot do it yourself. You need to load this form with information because schools have become vigilant in monitoring who is authorized to perform this service. Be creative in building your safety net. Many parents use co-workers, neighbors, and members of their church family who are willing to help out.

Make copies of this form before you turn it in to keep handy. Keep one at home, in your car, at work, and in your purse or wallet. Refer to it occasionally to see if you need to update any names, phone numbers, etc.

Health History

Make a list of approximate dates regarding significant illnesses and injuries, and any pervasive problems such as allergies. Be prepared with information about the birth of your child that could have a negative impact on normal development such as a premature delivery or an emergency C-section that was necessary due to fetal distress.

Dates of Developmental Milestones

If you have diligently kept a baby book, then you could receive an unexpected payoff. Extensive health information will be requested to see if developmental rates have been on target. You should be completely honest about any delays because the staff will use the information to remain alert to any potential physical, mental, or social problems they may need to attend to. Without this supporting information, they may not be able to justify the extra cost of utilizing needed specialists. Some examples are the approximate age in years and months when he or she:

> ➢ Completed potty training.
> ➢ Started crawling and walking.
> ➢ Said first words and then began putting sentences together.
> ➢ Began eating without assistance.

Medications and Dosage

The days of sending a few pills to school in a zip-lock sandwich bag are long gone. Students are rarely permitted to carry any medications with them during the school day. Whether prescribed, or just an over-the-counter drug, you must provide the school nurse with the original container specifying the directions for administration. Be sure to report the exact dosage of any medications taken regularly at home. This information needs to be kept on file in case your child would need to be treated during an emergency.

If you are parenting a child who can usually make a comeback after taking something for a headache or upset stomach, then ask if the nurse will keep a couple of doses on hand. It may save you a trip to school and more importantly, your child may be able to recover and finish the school day.

The information you provide will be protected as required by federal law.

Schools that receive funding for any program administered by the U.S. Department of Education must adhere to the Family Educational Rights and Privacy Act (FERPA), which protects the privacy of student records.[7] In a nutshell, only school officials and legally authorized people with a legitimate interest may review student records. If you would like detailed information about this law, you may call the U.S. Department of Education, Family Policy Compliance Office, at 1-800-877-8339 or visit their website at www.ed.gov.[8]

How to Decide If Your Child is Truly Ready

As recently as a decade ago, you could have been the worst parent in the world and sent your kid to kindergarten and no one would have known the difference. Schools were still teaching the basics—how to play nice, put your toys away, and wait quietly in a single-file line. Kindergarten was a year during which teachers had the chance to even out the playing field. Those who were a little behind in skills, such as identifying colors or counting, had a chance to catch up. Then someone yelled:

Oh no! Japan and other scary countries are turning out these genius kids that are going to take over the world with their inventions and technological stuff. We must add academics to kindergarten and get ahead!

Well, that's not exactly what happened, but over the years, kindergarten has become so academically challenging that you should not feel one bit ashamed if you choose to hold your child out for another year. You have that right as well as the right to make the decision to go ahead. There is no "passing mark" in screening results. The only real requirement is that you meet the birth date deadline set by the district. If you don't, you can contest the age requirement, but please don't. I have yet to meet an underage child who was socially, emotionally, physically, and cognitively ready to start school. In fact, I would wait another year just to avoid the hassle of having to figure out what to do if my child began to lag behind the others.

Nevertheless, I am not you, and I don't know your child personally, so show up for screening with the proper paperwork in hand anyway. When testing is completed, school professionals will use the results and the recommendations of those conducting the battery of tests to give you an expert opinion one way or the other. You may or may not receive a written report on that day, but when you do, you can revisit the information in this book to help you decide what to do. If you still have doubts, contact the school and ask to meet with the best qualified staff members to help you make an informed decision.

The question should not be: *Should I or shouldn't I go through the screening process?* Your focus should be on finding out whether or not your child has the capabilities to be successful in school, and if not, what weaknesses need to be addressed while sitting out for another year. Participating in the screening process should give you this information.

Most children who aren't ready for kindergarten are perfectly normal.

The majority who are not ready aren't deficient in any way except for "time." They simply need more time for their bodies and/or brain functioning to develop. Some telltale signs are:

> ➤ Has trouble finding the right words to ask a simple question or tell you what he or she needs.
> ➤ Can't retell a simple story or recall an event in a way that makes sense.
> ➤ Still needs assistance in the bathroom, and/or is afraid of using public restrooms.
> ➤ Is significantly smaller, weaker, and/or uncoordinated than others in the same age group.
> ➤ Prefers playing with younger children and/or has problems socializing with children of the same age group.
> ➤ Still needs a daytime nap.
> ➤ Can't sit still in church, in a restaurant, during story time at the library, or other public places for very long. When you force the issue, he or she either throws a fit or squirms and whines, interrupting the event.
> ➤ Seems to take forever to eat a meal.
> ➤ Doesn't pick up on cues in serious situations and continues to act "silly."
> ➤ Doesn't easily "separate" from you.

This type of development should not, or cannot, be rushed, so do not try to second guess what you are doing wrong as a parent.

Simple, self-maintenance skills should be mastered before starting school.

Are you still zipping, snapping, and buttoning clothes; tying shoes; opening and closing doors; and waiting outside the bathroom to assist with hygiene? Even though it is tempting to help speed things up, get it done right, or show affection, you need to stop so that these tasks can be mastered before entering school. It can be embarrassing to have to ask for assistance, especially when your friends are self-sufficient. Worse yet, it can be a huge bummer watching everyone charge out the door for recess when you can't go until someone helps you with your coat, hat, and mittens.

Be on the lookout for additional things you can do to encourage self-sufficiency. Fast food restaurants are a great place to practice carrying a tray, opening condiment packets, and cleaning up after oneself. Underdeveloped reflexes can mean many spills and subsequently having to withstand wet and messy clothing until the end of the school day.

Of lesser importance, but still an issue, I'd reconsider sending a bed-wetter to school if I had the option to hold out for another year. Even though it wouldn't have a direct effect on school performance, the social stigma can be devastating. Even if it is kept secret, it can have a negative effect on self-esteem knowing that others can participate in sleepovers and you can't. (The new "protective" underwear are great for younger kids, but this age group can immediately spot them.)

Are you worried that waiting out another year might not help?

The professionals involved during the first screening will certainly detect any potential problems and should make suggestions for waiting out another year worth it. Depending upon the resources available in your area and the detected weaknesses, those suggestions may include something as complex as finding a pediatric neurologist who specializes in behavior disorders, or something as simple as arranging time away from you to help curb separation anxiety.

If you are not alerted to any potential problems after the first screening other than just needing another year to mature, and then the second screening doesn't go very well, you should certainly ask about special services. Having a bad screening experience is not always a predictor of failure, but you should certainly be concerned.

Other Considerations

Some parents are afraid that their "intellectually gifted children" will be bored if they wait out another year. Research shows that smart children cannot use their intelligence very effectively if they are too immature to handle the structure and/or physical and social demands of school.[9] It doesn't matter how intelligent a child is, he or she may feel intimidated by bigger kids who seem to fit into social circles more easily. Younger students are also overpowered by their more physically developed and more coordinated peers. They often have to wait for an open piece of playground equipment and are shunned in games that require advanced agility. Unfortunately, the No Child Left Behind Act doesn't provide any kind of help for feeling "left behind" when your classmates are losing teeth and removing their training wheels and you're not.[10]

Kindergartners who are socially and physically immature may also suffer in other ways that parents fail to foresee. Crowded hallways can appear frightening to the smallest students, to say the least, even when everyone is behaving. Although bus drivers may assign seats and try to enforce rules to alleviate some of the aggressiveness that takes place, it is again the "runts of the litter" who get the worst of it. Students lugging backpacks, gym bags, and musical instruments inadvertently cause bumps and bruises, and when your feet do not touch the floor, you're sure to get jostled around. Other potentially traumatizing situations are the high noise levels in the cafeteria, the chaos at the end of the day when everyone is leaving at the same time, and emergency drills.

There are also different stages, surges, and rates of brain development, especially in young children. Early success doesn't mean that this advanced type of cognitive functioning will continue to spike.[11] According to Dr. James Dobson, whom I consider to be the supreme expert in child development, the last neurological mechanism to develop is visual; therefore, until the brain is ready, it is virtually impossible for a child to learn to read and write no matter how much drilling and grilling you are willing to do.[12] (Check out his website, at www.FocusontheFamily.com, for loads of advice on parenting.)

Along the same lines, parents may confuse the ability to memorize large amounts of information with the ability to reason, process information, and problem solve—the latter being more important for success in school.[13] A better indicator of readiness for school is a child who is curious and enthusiastic about learning new things. Wanting to know why the dog doesn't go bald when shedding, while Grandpa does, is actually a better indicator of readiness than being able to recite the ABC's.

A child that is not yet equipped mentally and/or physically for kindergarten may be facing an uphill climb for years to come. To further help you make an informed decision, ask to speak with a few seasoned elementary teachers about their experiences in working with children who were the youngest in their classes.

Is there a simpler way to predict readiness?

I believe that there are five qualities that typical, thriving kindergartners possess. Some students *never* acquire all five, or even one, but those who do appear to me to be having a wonderful time in school.

➢ Wants to be good, and prefers operating under a clear set of rules.
➢ Likes having a daily routine, and takes pride in knowing what to do next without prompting.
➢ Is eager to help others.
➢ Works hard to receive compliments.
➢ Is curious, and loves to learn new things.

How long can you wait?

Each state has its own "compulsory attendance law" which mandates when a child must begin school, and some permit individual districts a little leeway if they prefer to alter the date by a few months. The most commonly prescribed age for screening is five, but be sure you have accurate information well in advance, especially if you are planning to relocate.[14]

What if you can't afford pre-school?

My source of kindergarten teachers tell me that it is obvious which students have attended pre-school because of their ability to quickly adapt to the structure and rules of a classroom. That doesn't mean that other students are at a disadvantage in the long run. Even if you are a stay-at-home parent or utilize private day care, you can still provide the academic stimulation and socialization needed to ensure school success. My aim is to help you hit that mark.

If you suspect any developmental delays, or if you are economically disadvantaged, you may qualify for free services provided by an early intervention program in your geographical area. Contact your local educational service center or health department for information.

Paying for another year of childcare or pre-school may be worth the cost when you consider the emotional cost of parenting a struggling student for years to come.

A final thought:

Consider the gamble. Starting too soon may mean having to hustle to keep up. Waiting out a year could mean the chance to become a class front-runner.

All about Screening

The following information should take some of the mystery out of why we are so concerned about the inability to balance on one foot for at least 10 seconds, or why it is such a big deal to be able to find a rabbit with a missing ear in a picture. There is a reason for everything, even if it is just to see if we can pry the two of you apart for awhile. No matter how painful you find this, you must remember that we do not need to screen you—just your child. It is impossible to get a true measure of abilities if you are providing personal coaching.

Basic Communication Skills

A big part of assessing maturity during kindergarten screening involves listening as well as speaking.

Receptive Skills

This is a measure of how well a child understands what is heard. Being able to respond to simple questions and instructions is a good sign of readiness for school.

Expressive Skills

We are not looking for perfect grammar or enunciation; just the ability to say things that make sense.

Speech

Some parents do not realize just how much of a negative effect poor articulation can have on academic performance. Please remember that you have the advantage of being able to understand your child because you have grown accustomed to interpreting the same incorrect sounds over and over. Teachers are not always so lucky. The teacher/student relationship may become strained when it is hard to understand what a child is trying to communicate. More importantly, it may be difficult to fairly assess what a student has learned.

Whoever does the screening will identify recurring, incorrect sounds and be able to determine what might need to be corrected with therapy, and what may be outgrown. Many children will correct sounds as they mature and gain control over their tongue and facial muscles, which is reason enough for holding out a child for another year. Consult with the school speech therapist to be sure. In the meantime, encourage, but don't drill, correct pronunciation of words.

<u>Hearing</u>

Speech therapists are trained to screen for hearing problems in addition to poor articulation. Some speech problems are caused by the inability to imitate sounds because they are not heard correctly in the first place. Hearing problems can also be more than just a detriment to learning. Students who are continually frustrated often exhibit behavior problems as well.

You should report a suspected hearing problem immediately to your pediatrician, but don't panic. According to the National Institute on Deafness and Other Communications Disorders, hearing loss is typically related to, or caused by, a cold, ear infection(s), allergies, fluid in the ears, or swollen tonsils and/or adenoids. Most problems can be treated with medication or routine surgery.[15] I'm sure your health care provider will refer you if necessary, to a specialist.

Whether a hearing loss is temporary or permanent, the school is required by federal law to provide help during the school day to keep your child on track. The Individuals with Disabilities Education Act (IDEA) specifically requires that students with disabilities receive individualized curriculum, instruction, and supportive devices as needed.[16]

What can you do to boost communication skills?

This is one of the easiest areas to hone because there isn't much thinking or planning involved. Basically, all you have to do is start talking and listening as if you've just met a new friend.

> ➢ Too many adults treat children as if they were inanimate objects instead of human beings with thoughts and opinions. Initiate meaningful conversations, even if it's something as simple as how icky that frog looked after someone ran over it in the driveway. *(Did it hurt? It probably died so fast it didn't feel it.)*

➢ As painful as it can sometimes be, bite your tongue to allow your little one time to formulate thoughts into words. Do not jump in and finish his or her sentences.

➢ Don't spend an inordinate amount of time trying to "guess" what your child needs or wants. Being able to clearly and quickly communicate personal needs to the teacher is ultra important, so put your energies into coaching how to verbalize those needs.

➢ Cut out the baby talk. Ask, *Do you need to use the restroom?* instead of *Do you have to pee-pee?*

➢ Encourage mature sentence structure by modeling. If you've been asking, *All done?* after a meal, ask instead, *Are you finished eating? Would you like to be excused?*

➢ Children are most likely to mimic their parents, so concentrate on using good grammar, good diction, and eliminate profanity from your vocabulary.

➢ Verbalize your thoughts and actions. Children are brimming with innocent enthusiasm to learn about the world around them. *It rained pretty hard last night. That means I won't need to water my flowers. I'll bet the water in your swimming pool is deeper!*

➢ Instead of dragging a bored kid around, be engaging. *Let's go to the produce section and see if we can find some fruit you might like to eat. Since I need to stop by the bank later on, would you like to put part of the money Grandma gave you into your savings account?* ("Assist" at the bank, but don't do the talking or handle the passbook or money.)

➢ Encourage the sharing of thoughts and ideas by not being judgmental (unless you feel it is necessary). *This is my favorite time of the day. I love it when we all get to sit down and eat together and talk. What is your favorite time of the day?*

➢ Play question and answer games. Car rides are the perfect setting for asking silly, but thought provoking questions. *If you could keep any animal in the world in our backyard, what would it be and why? How would you take care of it? What kind of food would you feed it?*

➢ Practice giving two- and three-step instructions such as, *Please put your books back on the shelf, put your shoes on, and then go outside and tell Daddy that dinner is ready.*

Visual Discrimination

This is a test of the ability to see the differences in things, such as the rabbit with the missing ear. This is a function of the brain that develops with maturity, not something that can be "fixed" with glasses. It is important to be able to quickly recognize the differences in shapes, colors, sizes, patterns, and positioning because good visual discrimination must be developed in order to learn how to read. Reading is nothing more than constant and intensive visual discrimination.[17]

You should be able to see this skill developing as you read together and examine the accompanying pictures. (*How many monkeys are in the tree? Which one has the longest tail? Which one is the smallest?*) There are also a multitude of toys and games that involve recognition and sorting, available wherever toys are sold.

Vision

The Individuals with Disabilities Education Act ensures that students with serious vision problems get the help they need, but this does not include children who simply need to wear glasses. If you suspect a problem before or during screening, don't hesitate to see an optometrist. You should also be careful not to confuse shyness with poor eyesight. A child may erroneously appear to be timid when he or she cannot see what others are referring to and clams up.

According to the American Optometric Association, every child should receive an eye examination prior to starting school anyway, especially if poor vision runs in your family and/or if you observe any of the following red flags:

> ➢ Holding books close to the face.
> ➢ Sitting close to the TV.
> ➢ Squinting.
> ➢ Closing or covering one eye to see better.
> ➢ Avoiding detailed activities such as coloring or puzzles.
> ➢ Complaining of headaches or rubbing eyes when doing "close up" activities.
> ➢ Has extremely poor hand-eye-body coordination.[18]

Children have enough of an uphill climb adjusting to school without having to get used to wearing glasses at the same time, so don't delay.

(Suggested reading: *Blues Clues: Magenta Gets Glasses!* by Deborah Reber, or *Luna and the Big Blur: A Story for Children Who Wear Glasses* by Shirley Day.)

Gross Motor Skills

Some parents fail to see why it is necessary for us to "test" the ability to control the large muscles of the body. We are understandably interested in your child's ability to walk up and down stairs without falling, being able to stand in line without setting off a falling domino effect, and being able to balance a cafeteria tray right side up, but there is something much more important at stake. You must be able to control your large muscles in order to be able to develop fine motor skills.

Uncoordinated students have a difficult time mastering desk work. You must first be able to easily balance yourself while sitting normally in a chair, positioning yourself so that you're not using your arms as props. It is easy to provide opportunities to encourage development, but don't try to force your child to master something that his or her body is not physically prepared for. Instead, consider waiting out another year to encourage optimum physical strength and agility.

What if your child is a slug by nature?

Whatever you do, do *not* say, *You need to exercise.* That sounds like a prison sentence. Instead say, *You need to have more fun!* Provide a place indoors as well as outdoors where kids can be completely uninhibited without the fear of breaking something. Continue to cordon off your sitting room with red velvet theatre ropes if you must, but clean out the basement, back the cars out of the garage, or create some space in your yard, and then lead the charge. Just in case you've forgotten the sheer joy of unadulterated play, here are some suggestions:

> Ball games with age appropriate rules and equipment such as softball, basketball, touch football, and soccer. (Use plastic bats, balls made out of soft materials, smaller playing areas and lower nets.)
> Swimming
> Biking
> Hopscotch
> Walking—particularly race walking, running, walking backwards, hopping, and skipping.
> Hula-hooping
> Dancing
> Jumping rope (Look on the Internet for free descriptions of games and rhymes.)
> Roller skating/blading
> Backyard games such as hide-and-seek, tag, freeze tag, kick the can, and Red Rover.

If you invest in any video games, look for interactive versions that involve physical movement. Many games are designed so that all ages can enjoy them while getting a workout. (Two of my personal favorites are simulating playing games with the Nintendo Wii and any of the *Dance Dance Revolution* games made by several different companies.)

(Suggested reading: *Get Moving with Grover* by Random House, *Sidewalk Games* by Glen Vecchione, *Anna Banana: 101 Jump Rope Rhymes* by Joanna Cole, and *Mom's Handy Book of Backyard Games* by Pete Cava.)

Fine Motor Skills

The most important result of developing control over the small muscle groups of the hands and fingers is being able to print legibly. Developing strength and dexterity in the fingers of the dominant hand are necessary in order to use writing tools with control and intention. You can encourage this fine motor control, or "pincer grip" as it is often referred to by professionals, with the following activities:

> ➢ Putting together puzzles.
> ➢ Sorting small items.
> ➢ Playing with play dough or kneading real dough in the kitchen.
> ➢ Stringing beads.
> ➢ Cutting with safety-edge scissors.
> ➢ Drawing, tracing, or coloring.
> ➢ Playing games with small pieces.
> ➢ Playing with a plant sprayer outside or in the bathtub.
> ➢ Picking up coins and other small items without sliding them to the edge of the table.
> ➢ Dressing and undressing dolls.
> ➢ Printing. Make sure you encourage using the correct grip, the correct stroking direction—such as a down stroke for the letter "l"—and how to work from left to right across the page. There are many inexpensive booklets and free, downloadable worksheets available on the Internet that utilize arrows to show which direction to guide the hand. (Check out the chapter entitled *A Word about Learning to Print* before you begin.)

Learning to grasp and control eating utensils is a little less important, but should be mastered at least to the point where more food is ingested than ends up being worn. Students severely lacking in this area may go hungry if they will not attempt to eat anything that requires using a spoon or fork.

Early Academic Skills

This portion of the assessment will primarily measure knowledge of numbers, letters, and words. There are several types of professionally developed screening tests, but most involve repeating words, pointing to pictures, counting, and demonstrating number concepts (smaller, larger, half, whole, etc.). The score report should help you make an informed decision about the right time to begin school.

Typical Test Items

Again, there is no "passing mark" that qualifies a child for school. The level of knowledge and skills are not nearly as important as the ability to stay on task, grasp simple concepts, and appear enthusiastic about learning new things. The following list is a sampling of items that may be evaluated although no child is expected to have mastered everything prior to screening.

> ➢ Identify basic colors such as red, blue, green, yellow, orange, black, white, brown, purple, and pink.
> ➢ Count to 10 or higher in order. (Called "rote counting.")
> ➢ Count up to 10 objects. (Called "rational counting.")
> ➢ Count two groups of objects to determine which has "more or less."
> ➢ Demonstrate the concept of adding and/or subtracting by using five or less manipulatives. ("Manipulatives" are learning tools that you physically handle. An example of such a test would be asking the child to place three blocks into a box. The screener then asks the child to add more, remove some, all the while asking how many remain.)
> ➢ Recognize and copy basic shapes (circle, square, triangle, oval, rectangle, and diamond).
> ➢ Sort items according color, size, or shape.
> ➢ Demonstrate the ability to "sequence" items, such as arranging items in order from smallest to largest.
> ➢ Recognize name in print.
> ➢ Say and print first and last name.
> ➢ Say middle name.
> ➢ Say parents' first and last names.
> ➢ Say where parents work.
> ➢ Say age and birthday.
> ➢ Recite address and phone number.
> ➢ Follow a two- or three-step direction after hearing it once. (Put the ball in the box, the pencils in the cup, and the paper in the tray.)

- ➤ Recite the alphabet.
- ➤ Point to specific letters in print.
- ➤ Copy or print letters.
- ➤ Recognize rhyming words.
- ➤ Recite the days of the week.
- ➤ Respond correctly to questions about the concept of yesterday, today, and tomorrow.
- ➤ Identify self as a boy or a girl.
- ➤ Point to and say the names of basic body parts (head, mouth, ears, eyes, nose, arms, elbows, wrists, fingers, waist, hips, legs, knees, toes, heels, etc.)
- ➤ Show awareness of spatial relationships. (Is the book "under" or "on" the table? Is it "in front, inside, or behind" the box?)
- ➤ Sit quietly and listen to a story.
- ➤ Listen when spoken to and respond in a socially appropriate way. ("Hello. How are you?" *Fine, thank you.*)

(Suggested reading: *The Very Hungry Caterpillar* by Eric Carle, which covers the days of the week, numbers, and a taste of sequencing; *White Rabbit's Color Book* by Alan Baker; the *Icky Bug* books by Jerry Pallotta, focusing on letters, shapes, and numbers; and *I Knew Two Who Said Moo: A Counting and Rhyming Book* by Judi Barrett.)

Cheat Sheet for Understanding Test Scores

Since the inception of the No Child Left Behind Act, schools are now held accountable for every child's educational growth, so you can expect to be presented with a test report on a yearly basis.[19] It doesn't matter what type of testing your district administers, or what grade level is tested, the basic lingo is all the same.

Standardized Test

This is not the typical test that a teacher rips out of a workbook and runs through a copy machine. Standardized tests are a big deal and are given once or twice a year in order to provide the school and parents with some very important information:

> ➤ You will be able to see how your child's score compares to what has been determined to be the average score of a typical student who is the same age and/or in the same grade.
> ➤ The school will be able to analyze test results to see if changes need to be made in what is taught, or how it is taught, to maximize student achievement.
> ➤ Parents and appropriate school employees will be able to pinpoint individual weaknesses that need to be addressed aggressively to keep their children/students on grade level in all areas.

Your first experience with a standardized test will probably be during kindergarten screening.

Professionals do not guess at whether or not your child is ready to begin school. They will carefully consider a host of factors, the most important being the results of such a test. Schools have the option of using several different forms that have been developed by experts who have collaborated, experimented, and refined what they believe to be predictors of what skills enable a kindergartner to be successful.

Be careful not to create a sense of panic.

Prior to kindergarten screening, and every important test that comes along after this one, you should avoid inducing the wrong kind of hype in your household. You will probably receive some kind of notification on a regular basis of all the things you should do, i.e., make sure your child gets a good night's sleep, eats a hearty breakfast, and dresses in layers, but more importantly, you want to alleviate or prevent unhealthy pressure to do well. There will be enough of that turmoil to deal with when you start college admission testing. For now, you might explain the purpose of the test in this way:

It's just a test to see how you're doing.

Rather than…

This is a test to see who is the smartest in the class!

A poor performance is not the end of the world, especially during kindergarten screening. Standardized tests fail to take into consideration important factors such as constipation, dying gold fish, and having on that hot itchy sweater you hate. An extremely poor performance during screening, however, should not be ignored, especially if you expected better results. Soaring intelligence means nothing if there are serious problems with social and/or physical maturity that prevents your child from demonstrating what he or she knows. Don't wonder what went wrong. Ask for a professional opinion.

There are two basic types of standardized tests:

Aptitude Test

It measures the ability to learn. It is a predictor of academic success so educators can plan curriculum to maximize a student's potential. These are commonly used to see if students need academic enrichment, such as a "Talented and Gifted Program," or as part of an assessment to determine if a student is in need of special education services.

Achievement Test

Also referred to as "Criterion-Referenced Tests," they are designed to measure how much a student has already learned. These tests are becoming more common than any other type of test in response to the government's push to turn out students who have mastered material in academic subjects such as reading, writing, math, science, and social studies. How are these tests compiled?

> Your State Department of Education is responsible for coming up with "state standards," which are all the things students should be learning in school, such as how to read fluently.
> Next, they come up with "content standards," which are the specific things students should know or be able to do in individual subject areas at each grade level. An example for kindergarten would be "demonstrate phonemic awareness" which is the ability to recognize the individual sounds of a word.
> The next step is to decide just how well students should know these things by creating "performance standards," which determine "how good is good enough." For example, kindergartners are expected to be able to apply phonemic awareness by being able to sound out words that should be mastered at this grade level.
> To prevent teachers from having to "guess" if their students are making progress along the way, they are provided with "benchmarks." Collectively, these serve as a reliable gauge so they'll know whether or not their students are "getting it." A simple example would be the benchmark of being able to "identify random letters of the alphabet" before learning to sound out words.
> Lastly, once tests are compiled, guidelines for test administrators are created, such as time limits to ensure the validity of scores.

What type of test will be used during kindergarten screening?

Screening tests are generally a combination of both, measuring aptitude and achievement. We want to know what each child already knows, but more importantly, we need to get a good read on whether or not potential students are ready to learn.

National Percentile Rank

This is a "comparison" score. For example, if the student's rank is 80, then he or she scored better than approximately 80 percent of typical test takers and worse than 20 percent. Fifty is not a terrible score; it means your child is average.

Stanine

Similar to the National Percentile Rank, students are compared, but only on a scale of 1 to 9. A score of 1, 2, or 3 is considered below average; 4, 5, or 6 is in the average range, and 7, 8, or 9 indicates an above average performance. These scores are typically used when a test is divided into subtests.

Subtests

These are sections of a test that can be scored separately to reveal specific weaknesses and strengths. Maybe the test taker has the ability to read exceptionally well, but can't write worth a lick. In this case, the reading score would be high and the writing score low.

Raw Score

This is the total number of correct answers. There could be a hundred items on the test, or a thousand; it doesn't matter. The raw score is how many questions the student answered correctly.

Mean

This is the average score. Your report should tell you what group of test takers is included in this average. For instance, if the test was given state-wide, it may include every single test taker so you can see how your child compares.

Standard Deviation

This is a number that determines how far away from the mean a student's score falls. If the majority of test scores are close to the mean, but a student's score falls way below, that student performed poorly. Conversely, the higher the score falls above the mean, the better the performance.

Standard Score

This score enables you to see just how good a test score is according to a reliable comparison to previous test takers.

Norms

These are an explanation of what scores mean such as what range of scores are "normally" attained by low, average, and high achievers.

Grade Equivalent

This is an indication of how a student compares to other students at different grade levels. For example, a student who scores 1.3 in reading comprehension is able to read and understand at the level expected of a student who has been in first grade for three months. A score of 2.4 is a performance expected of a second grader in the fourth month of school, and so on.

Age Equivalent

Similar to "grade equivalent," this is a comparison to other students, but it is based on chronological age. A score of 6-8 would reflect that the student's performance is typical of a child who is six years and eight months old.

Difficulty Index

Sometimes test reports will go so far as to tell you which questions were hard and which ones were easy. The ratings generally include at least three categories which might be termed "easy, of medium difficulty, and hard." These ratings are determined by the percentage of students who answered the questions correctly on that particular test. In other words, if the percentage of students who answered a question correctly is high, then that particular question will be rated as "easy."

IQ

IQ is an acronym for Intelligence Quotient, which was originally based on a formula developed to calculate one's intelligence level. The mental age, as determined by testing, is divided by the chronological age and multiplied by 100. Over the years, IQ tests have evolved somewhat, but the basic premise is still the same. These tests are designed to measure how a child's learning potential compares to other children who are the same age.

Even though many schools have eliminated a great deal of this type of aptitude testing to make way for mandated achievement testing in specific subject areas, various forms are still utilized quite frequently such as the Stanford-Binet. They are most often used by school psychologists who test for suspected learning disabilities, and the professionals who are responsible for determining which students qualify for talented and gifted programs.[20]

If you receive test results that include an "IQ" or "School Ability Index" score, you will be provided with a scale specifically designed for the particular test given. IQ scales vary slightly depending upon the source you consult, but the one developed by Psychologist Lewis M. Terman in 1916 still serves as a reliable interpretation.[21]

20-34 = Severe Mental Retardation
35-49 = Moderate Retardation
50-69 = Mild Mental Retardation
70-79 = Borderline Deficiency in Intelligence
80-89 = Dullness
90-109 = Average or Normal Intelligence
110-119 = Superior Intelligence
120-140 = Very Superior Intelligence
Over 140 = Genius or almost Genius

Please keep in mind that this is just one number that is determined without consideration of the many variables that effect student success: teacher effectiveness, parent involvement, environmental influences, peer pressure, maturity, the availability of intervention and enrichment programs, the will (or lack of) to succeed academically, and your emotional and physical state during testing.

Shopping for School Clothes

The following suggestions are meant to help you dress your child appropriately for comfort and ease in participating in daily activities. Hopefully you will also be able to save some money by knowing what *not* to buy.

Check out the school dress code.

Most school districts adopt a dress code that all students must adhere to. Even though a kindergartner wearing a Hooters T-shirt wouldn't have the slightest idea that the graphics were representative of anything other than a friendly-looking hoot owl, said student is probably going to end up in the principal's office. I'm sure you don't want school employees to think that you are a parent who encourages rebel-like behavior, so save suggestive apparel for your family reunions.

To avoid having to take time out of your busy day to swing by the school with a change of clothing, be sure that you know the rules about how much skin can be exposed. Spaghetti straps, belly shirts, and mini skirts are typically a big no-no.

You may not agree with the dress code, but each and every rule has been borne out of a situation that has created a problem that has somehow interrupted what educators refer to as "the educational process." For instance, when it was discovered that bandanas were being worn to show allegiance to certain gang sects, most schools banned students from wearing any kind of scarf.

Look for "all-purpose" shoes.

Think about how you choose a new pair of shoes to wear to work. Unless you work for a circus, you expect to walk normally in them—not run, jump, skip, or hop. You do not anticipate that someone will be stepping on them every five minutes either. Now that you're getting the picture, you should also consider the following shopping tips.

> Check the bottoms for stability. Avoid slippery soles and raised or pointy heels.

> Avoid buying shoes with skinny, satiny shoelaces that won't stay tied. If you can't resist the shoes, buy old-fashioned flat shoe strings that are easier to manage and swap them. Choose ones that are short enough so they won't drag the ground even if tied in uneven loops. If this skill hasn't been mastered before starting school, then buy "slip on" shoes or shoes with Velcro closures.

> If you're buying anything other than tennis shoes, feel the interior so you can avoid buying shoes with places that might "rub." Make sure they are broken in before school begins, or buy them big enough so that socks can be worn.

> Don't forget to make a plan for bad weather. It is a horrible feeling to have to sit in class with wet feet, so send an extra pair of dry shoes and socks to change into. Sending an extra pair of shoes is just as important for kids who wear boots. It is tiring to have to lug your hot, sweaty feet around in boots all day long. Whether you purchase "over the shoe" boots or boots that are worn alone, make sure they aren't so tight that they are hard to get on and off.

> Don't buy backless shoes. There are two basic differences between elementary students and junior high/high school students when it comes to P.E. class. Elementary students do not have to change clothes and they actually look forward to the class. Backless shoes slow kids down, and the likelihood of blowing out a flip-flop increases considerably when you are running. If that isn't convincing enough, schools in my area banned them after learning that a student in a neighboring district broke her leg when someone stepped on the back of her shoe and she fell down a flight of stairs.

> Don't buy shoes with built in "skates" for school. They are becoming the latest forbidden fruit of fashion in student handbooks.

Forget buying ruffles, bows, designer duds, or anything that can't be thrown in the washer.

One of the most endearing traits of elementary students is their obliviousness to social status. If someone looks desperately poor, no one cares. If you are fun to play with, that's all that really matters. It's that simple. And forget about trying to impress the staff by sending a perfectly groomed kid to school. They'll be far more impressed by a book bag that contains completed homework and lunch money.

Another reason for shunning high price tags is that you will more than likely be mortified at what can happen to brand new clothing in just one day. With the muck to wallow in on the playground, sloppy art projects, and lunchtime mishaps, you'd be better off using your extra cash to buy stock in companies that manufacture stain remover. Besides, before you know it, you'll have a teenager wearing down the numbers on your credit card while begging for all the latest styles.

Don't forget that stores are open year round.

Don't go crazy. Just buy enough stuff so that you can keep up with the laundry. Kids don't get snotty about seeing one another in the same outfit twice in one week until middle school. And just as soon as you think you're set for the year, your kid will outgrow everything. My sister Jane Ann's mathematical theory about growth spurts explains it all:

The number of pairs of jeans you buy is in direct proportion to the number of inches your child will grow the same week of your purchase.

Identify everything with an indelible pen.

When you go shopping for school supplies, add this to your list. Choose one with a fine tip so you can write legibly on small labels inside clothing that may be removed during the school day. Be sure you are buying "indelible" ink to prevent fading in the wash. You can also use it to mark other items that may not find their way home again, such as book bags and lunch boxes.

Periodically check the "lost and found."

Year after year, the piles of unclaimed clothing, toys, lunch boxes, and book bags that are left behind never cease to amaze me. Try to keep track of what goes out of your house in the morning and then what makes it back. A lost mitten, a few hair barrettes, and a forgotten sweater may not seem like much, but over the course of 13 years of school, the money you lose will add up. Plus, school employees get tired of shuffling around mounds of lost items which eventually have to be hauled away to a local charity.

Schools *welcome* parents who want to search for things they've purchased with their hard-earned cash. You should never feel sheepish for doing so.

And do we worry that people will do a little "shopping" in our bins? We don't have to because we know that most children will immediately spot their property on someone else's back.

"Gear up" for cold weather.

Most schools have outdoor temperature guides for requiring coats, hats, and mittens for recess. Students who do not have what is required will be kept indoors. You can solve the hat problem by buying a hooded coat. Look for hoods that have Velcro or snap closures at the chin or are gathered with elastic to stay in place so you won't have to worry about the safety hazards of a drawstring. They can easily get caught in bus doors and on playground equipment, so if you purchase a coat that has one, remove it! If you choose a coat without a hood, buy several inexpensive hats to keep on hand.

The same goes for mittens. Don't be tempted to buy "idiot" mittens that are connected by a string or attached to coat sleeves with elastic. Besides being dangerous, in no time at all they'll start looking like dangling road kill, so you'll end up running for the scissors anyway.

Your best bet is to tuck an extra hat and mittens in a separate compartment of your child's backpack.

Buy a coat that is easy to zip.

For added convenience, occasionally spray the zipper with a little WD-40.

Avoid any accessories that can get caught in doors, playground equipment, or even hair.

I cannot emphasis enough that you shouldn't buy belts, sashes, necklaces, dangly jewelry or anything with attached strings.

Do not adorn clothing with cutesy noisemakers.

As much fun as it is to attach jingly bells to shoelaces at Christmas time, or novelty buttons to shirts that rudely blare messages (my least favorite being, *Who's your daddy!*), don't do it. It only adds to the chaos.

Send a complete change of clothing that can be tucked away for emergencies.

Buy something cheap or send an outfit that is pretty much worn out, but still loose-fitting, because it may never be used. The occasional accident usually involves one of the following.

> ➢ Not making it to the bathroom. (If the odds aren't very good to begin with, buy elastic waist pants.)
> ➢ Wrecking attire at lunch time.
> ➢ Throwing up on oneself or being on the receiving end of someone else's projectile vomiting.
> ➢ Getting wet at recess or taking a good tumble in the mud.
> ➢ Getting soaked on the way to school by an unexpected cloudburst.

"Bibs" are cute (meaning pants with buckled straps), but don't buy them for school.

Waiting in line for a stall can be excruciating enough, let alone having to fumble with the buckles. Even if you profess to be parenting a "master of bibs," I guarantee that if the straps don't end up in the toilet, they will at least drag across the crud on the floor during maneuvering.

Buy clothing that can be layered.

As difficult as it can be to predict the weather, it can be equally difficult to predict the temperature inside a school building. Regardless of the location of a child's classroom (top floors are generally the warmest rooms in the building), you should consider that during P.E., recess, or spending time in an air conditioned library, it would be nice to be able to add on or peel off clothing.

The bottom line:

Most kids don't care how they look; they just want to feel comfortable and have fun.

School Supplies

Shop together and treat the experience as if you are shopping for a special occasion. It will help your child look forward to starting school every year, knowing that he or she will be getting some new "stuff."

Thou shall not deviate from the teacher's list.

You will be provided with an easy-to-follow supply list during registration, so don't waste money by purchasing random items in advance. Avoid buying anything that is not needed as those things will only add clutter and unnecessary weight to a backpack. When children have too much stuff to contend with, they typically feel overwhelmed and give up on attempting to stay organized.

And lastly, stay in the good graces of the teacher by buying precisely what is on the list. For example, if you are asked to buy the basic box of 24 Crayola crayons, then don't buy a box of 64. There's a reason for everything. When it comes to crayons, the Crayola box of 24 includes all the colors that will be taught. (Even Crayola executives know if they want to stay in cahoots with kindergarten teachers, they had better never change anything about the basic box of 24.) If you want to buy a box of 64 because you can't resist all the groovy, interesting shades, then go ahead. Just keep them at home. A box of 64 only complicates things at school by adding more colors to fish through and may also intensify the temptation for others to go after your kid's crayons because they are "different."

Keep some extra supplies at home.

It will keep you from having to run to the store to replace items needed for school, and you'll always have what you need to complete homework.

Shopping for the Perfect Backpack

Before you make a purchase, find out if backpacks are prohibited and if they are, how students are expected to tote books and supplies. If you are limited to "see through" plastic, don't knock it because these are the cheapest models.

To make a functional choice, have your child lift it, put it on, and open and close each compartment. Avoid models with Velcro or snap closures which become faulty with bulk. Kids at this age have a better chance of keeping their goods intact with zipper closures, especially if you remember to periodically spray on a little WD-40 for ease of movement.

It is important that you note how heavy your choice is when empty. Too many gadgets and chambers may add unnecessary weight. Wheels are great, but remember there will still be times, such as climbing bus steps, when they are useless.

Most are durable enough to be thrown in the bathtub with some suds, or even hosed off outside. If you would rather not bother, then buy a cheaper model so you can replace it when it becomes too gross to bear.

Be meticulous about going through each compartment every night after school to check for homework assignments, messages from the teacher, and to reorganize and eliminate clutter. I also recommend that you buy a photo album or scrapbook that contains large plastic pockets so you can quickly slide in the work you want to keep. That way, you can see evidence of the progress being made throughout the year, plus, you'll have something sentimental to hang on to.

Classroom Supplies

Don't be surprised by requests for tissues, paper towels, and/or anti-bacterial wipes. Teachers can go broke trying to keep up with runny noses and spills.

Incidentally, if you, or any organization that you are affiliated with, would like to donate supplies for needy children (or children whose parents would rather spend their money on booze and cigarettes), please do. Schools will be glad to provide lists for anyone willing to help out, but you can score points with your child's teacher by simply buying a duplicate set of supplies. You can always add the amount to your "charitable contributions" on your tax return.

First Day Checklist

- Make sure everything is ready the night before to avoid the rush. Lunch or lunch money and supplies should be packed. Clothes, shoes, and accessories should all be placed in one spot. Make sure any money you're sending is the exact amount, placed in an envelope or sealable sandwich bag, and marked with your child's name and what it is for.
- If you've forgotten to break in new shoes, then choose another pair. Check to see that socks or tights are not too thick or too thin for comfort. The school nurse treats more blisters on the first day than any other time of the year.
- Review all the printed information you received during screening, registration, and orientation.
- Familiarize yourself with the school website and bookmark it in case you need to recheck information at the last minute. Later on, you should be able to access an academic progress report.
- If you haven't set up your "central command station" yet, now is the time. Hang up a copy of the district calendar as well as the names of radio and television stations that will carry any school related announcements such as delays or cancellations during inclement weather.
- The teacher will probably provide you with a name tag. If not, make your own. Include the correct bus number or other transportation information such as "parent pickup" and stick it on clothing the night before so you won't forget. If you are worried that the teacher will not remember something important such as a food allergy, write that information on the tag as well.
- If you have any less important messages for the teacher, write them down and place them with something else the teacher will be looking for such as lunch money or forms to be turned in.

> ➤ If you will be picking up your child, find out where you are to wait. Don't expect to be able to go directly to the classroom.

> ➤ For those who are riding the bus, review proper behavior. Make arrangements for someone trustworthy to walk your child to the bus stop if you can't do it yourself. Once you've scoped out the situation, you might be able to find someone who would be able to do this every day or share the job with you.

> ➤ If you live within walking distance, walk the route together several times beforehand to assess potential dangers. Emphasize safety, including obeying traffic lights, staying inside crosswalks, staying on the sidewalk, and watching out for drivers who are still moving even though you have a "walk" light.

> ➤ Don't forget to take a picture of this very important milestone. Taking a picture will help emphasize that this is a day to be celebrated, not feared, the same as taking pictures on birthdays and holidays. For the extremely skittish, invite extended family members, neighbors, and other significant people to come to your house and cheer the new student on!

> ➤ Don't send your child off to school too early. The anticipation of waiting for the bus or for school to begin can become very stressful, and more importantly, there may not be any supervision.

> ➤ When the two of you hook up again at the end of the day, don't misread a less than enthusiastic greeting. School can be exhausting, especially for a student who has been totally engaged in all the activities of the day, and more so at the beginning of the year. Ask how it went anyway so you'll know if you need to write a note to the teacher, send something you forgot, etc.

> ➤ Go through the backpack together. Was everything turned in? Did you get any notes, flyers, or newsletters from the teacher? Is there anything in there that belongs at school or to another child? Are there any homework assignments?

Taking the Mystery and Fear Out of the First Day

Very few people ever have much of a recollection of what the first day of kindergarten was like, but you no doubt remember the first day of something that was a little scary. Even adults who are looking forward to a new experience know how you're bound to have at least a few moments of heart-pounding apprehension about what you will be doing and what everything will be like. Just be careful not to let any of your own anxieties ruin what should be a positive experience.

Conduct your own orientation.

Being close to the familiar overrides fear, so in addition to the orientation put on by the school, you might want to stage your own "dress rehearsal." You can mimic a typical school morning, including traveling the path to and from school. If the school is open, stop and ask if you may see your child's classroom. If the teacher happens to be working, you might even drop off a small gift and say hello, but don't stay more than a minute. Preparations take a huge amount of time and effort.

If you haven't already done so, start building a network of adults who are likely to connect emotionally with your child.

The more adults who gravitate into your child's life, the better. The reason why I am mentioning it now is that adjusting to school is certainly easier for students who have lots of adult mentors. You can always find good role models among coaches, dance teachers, 4-H advisors, Sunday school teachers, and the like, but don't overlook other people whom, given the chance, would love to make a difference in a child's life. People outside your immediate family who dole out attention and encouragement just because they want to may stick around and become even more helpful when your teenager hates you and won't listen to anything you say.

Taking the time to discuss expectations will help make the transition into school much more pleasant for the both of you.

Here are some suggestions for answering typical questions prior to starting school. In addition, you should keep an upbeat dialog going now and then for reassurance that you have hit on every scary topic imaginable.

Who will take care of me?

Kindergartners often become frightened when they are supervised by teachers or school employees other than their regular classroom teachers. Prior to opening day, ask what additional people will be involved in your child's school day to tailor this explanation.

Your mommy and daddy take care of you at home, but your teacher will take care of you while you are at school, your bus driver while you are on the bus, your art teacher during art class, your music teacher during music class, etc.)

What is the first thing we will do?

Your teacher will probably show everyone where to sit and where to put their things. Then you might say the Pledge of Allegiance to the Flag, or the teacher will count how many students are buying their lunch and how many brought their lunch. I'm not sure what will happen first, but I am looking forward to hearing all about it when you get home.

What if I get into trouble because I don't know what to do?

Your teacher will tell you what the rules are and will help you when you don't know what to do. No one will remember everything the first day, and your teacher and other adults will remind you when you forget. You'll probably learn to stay in your seat until the teacher tells you to move somewhere else, you'll learn to stand in line and then walk quietly with your class to go places like the bathroom and cafeteria, and you'll learn to raise your hand and wait for the teacher to call your name before you talk.

What if I forget to raise my hand when I want to say something?

If you forget, the teacher will remind you. Why don't we practice raising our hands when we want to say something? Let's try it during dinner tonight for fun!

What if I have to go to the bathroom?

You will need to raise your hand and wait for the teacher to talk to you. Something that will help you a lot is to use the bathroom whenever the entire class goes, whether you feel like you need to or not.

What will we learn?

Some of the boys and girls will know more than you do, and some won't know as much as you. The teacher will have you practice the letters and numbers you have been learning at home, and a lot of other things. I can't wait to hear what you get to do every day.

Will it be hard?

Please be aware that a common fear is the mistaken belief that you must know how to read and write before you start school.

Your teacher will be very smart and will know how to help you learn so it doesn't seem hard. But don't worry if you can't do something. Mommy and Daddy can help you when you get home if you want, or the teacher will keep helping you until you can do it. Learning can be fun and will make you feel really proud of yourself!

What will be the best part?

You'll probably like making new friends the best, but you may like some other things too. Some boys and girls like playing games in gym class, some like drawing and making things in art class, some like going to the library and picking out books, and some like it when the teacher reads to the whole class. Some like playing learning games on the computer, some like singing in music class, some like learning new words, and some like lessons with numbers the best. I can't wait to hear what your favorite part of school is.

How will I get home?

At the end of the day, your teacher will make sure you get on the right bus, (or will make sure you're in the right place to be picked up, or escorted home, etc.).

(Suggested reading: *Billy and the Big New School* by Laurence Anholt, *Kindergarten Rocks* by Katie Davis, *Look Out Kindergarten, Here I Come* by Nancy Carlson, *Countdown to Kindergarten* by Alison McGhee, or *First Day Jitters* by Julie Danneberg.)

Developing Safety Plans

Children take tremendous pride in knowing exactly what to do when others are in doubt. For this reason, you shouldn't feel guilty about frequently quizzing your child about the safety plans that you develop. The information in this section should help you cover the basics, and help you figure out what else you need to do.

Early Dismissals

You'll be notified ahead of time about teacher's meetings and holidays, but there may be unannounced early dismissals when weather conditions or other emergencies occur. Kindergartners are far too young to be "latch key" kids, so make as simple a plan as possible that can be understood, remembered, and followed.

Review the plan often, asking questions such as, *Which bus do you ride to Grandma's house if you get out of school early? What do you do if Grandma isn't home? What is my phone number at work? What do you do if you get home from school and I'm not home?*

Write everything down for the school to keep on file and keep a copy in your child's backpack. You may or may not be able to get the bus driver to take a copy. Bus drivers must adhere to rules about where and when to drop off or pick up students. It is common for drivers to be instructed not to allow students to deviate from that rule unless they have a bus pass provided by the school, or a note from a parent. Nevertheless, when special circumstances occur, school employees need to feel confident that they are taking the right action. This is why it is imperative that you include important phone numbers! Practice getting it out of a special place in the backpack while saying, *If you don't know what to do, show this to the adult who is trying to help you.* It could mean the difference between picking up your child at your neighbor's house rather than the police station.

Illness

As previously stated, it is standard operating procedure for schools to keep a list of people on file who may be called to pick up your child if he or she is too ill to remain in school (typically called an "emergency medical form" that you'll fill out during registration). The longer the list, the better.

Keep a copy at home, at work, in your car, and in your purse or wallet. Then you will not have to worry about finding someone to intercept your child in a pinch, as well as being able to authorize emergency medical attention if needed.

Notify the school when you know your child will be absent.

School employees expect you to be just as responsible as you expect them to be in keeping track of your child. If you get into the habit of shirking your duty of calling in, then employees will probably learn to assume that you know why your child hasn't shown up for school. Schools are required to routinely check on those who are absent, but by the time attendance is taken and reported to the office, precious time has already passed in the event that something tragic has happened. Be diligent about calling in so we will be more apt to act quickly if you don't.

Send a follow-up note the next day to verify the absence.

Most schools require it, and If not, a note will ensure that the absence is recorded as legitimate.

What can you do as a parent for added safety?

Even though you should label everything with your child's name, don't do it conspicuously so that a predator could easily see it. Even though schools would like to believe that their security measures are invincible, nothing is fool proof. Students need to understand that they should not go anywhere in the building or outside the building unless "familiar" adults in charge know about it. This might be the teacher, bus driver, principal, nurse, or other employees that he or she sees on a regular basis.

For peace of mind and extra precaution, do the following things:

Come up with an unusual code word.

The old "your-mom-told-me-to-pick-you-up" trick is still successful far too often. Creeps often troll for kids on their way to or from bus stops, and some are even so brazen that they will hang around schools.

Practice repeating your phone number(s).

This is essential in case of some kind of transportation mix-up, or in the event that there has been an emergency at school and students have been evacuated to another location. When the two of you are out and about and you need to call your office or home, ask your child for the number to demonstrate how important it is to remember phone numbers.

Play the "what if" game.

For example, before a field trip, say: "What do you do if you get lost?" *Don't leave the building. Look for someone who works there and tell that person you are lost. If you are outside, go inside a building and look for someone who works there. If it is a house, stay on the porch and tell the person who answers the door to call your school or the police.* (The school can radio the bus driver or call the teacher's cell phone.) *If someone is using their telephone or cell phone to help you and you are scared, ask if you can call me.*

Talk about "good touches and bad touches."

Ideally you should introduce this topic before starting kindergarten, and preferably in a way that does not associate the idea directly with going to school. More than likely, there will be programs integrated into the curriculum, but don't wait for that to happen. Predators have an easy time with children who haven't gotten the word yet.

If you are worried about what to say, there are several wonderful children's books you can read together such as *It's My Body,* by Lory Freeman, and *The Right Touch,* by Sandy Kleven. There are also a multitude of websites that can guide you in your approach if you are worried about saying something that might be confusing or frightening. The best example I've seen is a short and simple online booklet entitled *Say No!* which was put together by the New York State Office of Children and Family Services, which is available at:

www.ocfs.state.ny.us/main/publications/Pub1154text.asp.[22]

My advice is to keep your discussions matter-of-fact, with the same attitude you would exhibit if you were talking about how to safely cross a street. The basic messages you should cover include:

➢ No one should touch any of your body parts that are covered by a bathing suit except for your doctor, or when Mommy or Daddy help you with your bath or put on a Band-Aid or something like that.

➢ Do not allow anyone else to talk you into touching his or her parts that are covered by a bathing suit.

➢ Your body belongs to you, so whenever someone touches you in any way that feels uncomfortable, you should speak up and say so right then and there!

➢ You should always tell Mommy and Daddy when someone has made you feel uncomfortable. We will always believe you even if it is someone we know really well.

➢ Touching should never be a secret. If someone tells you that they will hurt you or anyone else if you tell, don't be scared to tell us. We won't let that happen.

Check out the new "SafetyTat" tattoos.

These FDA approved, temporary tattoos were invented by Michelle Welch, a mother of three who came up with the idea after a nerve-wracking visit to an amusement park. She wrote her cell phone number on her kids' arms, worried about becoming separated, but the water rides and perspiration kept wearing away the ink. Very affordable for parents and schools, they can be custom ordered with phone numbers and even allergy alerts. Visit www. safetytat.com for more information.[23]

When you talk to your child about any serious issues, adjust your body so that you can make level eye contact, and hold both hands in yours.

These gestures will signal that what you're saying is extremely important. If you're asking for information, this will also increase the likelihood that you will get the truth. It doesn't matter if the conversation is negative or positive, once you've finished talking, you should end the conversation with a hug. That is the signal that you are finished and you love your child no matter what.

(Suggested reading: *Officer Buckle and Gloria* by Peggy Rathmann.)

Getting a Jump Start on Rules and Routines

Children who are used to predictable routines and moderate structure at home should be able to adjust quickly to the rules and procedures at school. For a seamless transition into the new school year, start making adjustments little by little throughout the summer. The first few weeks of school can be traumatic enough for little ones without the added shock of being constantly *corrected* or *redirected,* as teachers so politely put it these days. You know your child better than anyone else so for a smooth start, try to anticipate the problems that may occur and work on those.

(Suggested reading: *Lilly's Purple Plastic Purse* by Kevin Henkes.)

Start by adjusting bedtimes.

Long before you start working on a morning routine, you need to do your own "child study" to see just how many hours of sleep are needed in order to have an upright, conscious, and reasonably cooperative kid. In general, kindergartners need somewhere around 10-12 hours per night.[24] While you're at it, see if you can figure out what your requirements are as well. If you're rested, you'll have a lot more patience when the dog takes off with a sock or the bus driver zooms by because you're not standing on the curb.

Set up and follow a time table similar to a regular school day.

This is a necessity, especially for those who did not attend pre-school. Start by waking up and getting dressed at exactly the same time you will be getting ready for school a week or so beforehand. Set an egg timer and limit breakfast and lunch times to approximately 30 minutes to practice balancing out chatter and eating. Designate times for playing, reading together, bathing, and other activities to take the shock out of having to adhere to a structured day once school begins.

Resist the urge to continue playing the part of your child's personal assistant.

No matter how badly you want to jump to the rescue when it is obvious your child is struggling with self-management skills, don't do it. In order to function well in school, students need to be able to keep track of their own things, return classroom materials to their proper places, take care of business in the bathroom (including turning the water faucet on and off), manage zippers and buttons, tie their own shoes, and wipe their own noses. If you can hack it, you should even allow your child to practice carrying dishes to the sink. It can be an awfully long afternoon having to endure the feeling of sticky clothes and soupy socks and shoes, so I'd say this is one of the most important tasks to master. If you already know you'll be paying for school lunches, practice carrying food on a tray or partitioned plate at home, or when you're out for fast food.

Achieving self-reliance will build confidence which will in turn improve all areas of functioning in school. Waiting in line for help getting dressed for recess while your friends are already running free is depressing. It not only cuts into playtime, it becomes a demeaning event to be left behind with the other "babies." It is also irritating for school employees to have to waste valuable time tending to children who are perfectly capable of taking care of themselves. We know you mean well, but please restrain yourself from overdoing it.

Make rules for taking care of possessions.

This can be a helpful prelude to taking care of school supplies and other items that will have to be replaced if lost, stolen, or broken. Developing organizational skills will cut down on your work load as well.

> ➤ Every toy must be put away in its designated container or place before getting out another.
> ➤ Crayons and other writing tools are to be returned to their containers.
> ➤ Pick up and throw away all trash.
> ➤ Dirty clothes, shoes, jackets, wet towels, etc. should be put in their proper places. (Hang hooks and towel racks low enough to hit. Just don't be too fussy about placement.)

> ➤ Any pictures, papers, or artwork should either be thrown away or put in a specific place such as a box or drawer.

Demonstrate the importance of respecting others' property.

It is a continuous fight for school employees to teach kids to keep their mitts off of others' school supplies, food, loose articles of clothing, money, and toys brought to share during recess. Set a good example by asking before you dig through your wife's purse or husband's wallet, etc.

Use "teacher talk" whenever you can so it will become familiar.

For example, we should all use our *inside voices* when we are in our homes or other buildings. We can use our *outside voices* in the backyard and on the playground. *We should keep our hands to ourselves and take turns. Throwing sand is not acceptable; you need to make a better choice. You know the consequence for not putting your toys away. Respect others' property.*

Don't shun or make fun of the rules that your new student brings home. Incorporate them into your everyday lives and who knows, you might even entice your spouse into behaving a little better.

Talk the talk and walk the walk yourself.

Don't use foul language. If you do, maybe you're the one who needs to go sit in a corner so it will be evident that you know right from wrong. To this day, I can still see Mrs. Dyer's hair flying out of her bun as she stomped towards a boy in my class who said,

I can't find my spelling paper because my desk is a $*%#!$ mess!

Begin conducting your personal affairs under the assumption that there is no such thing as a family secret to a kindergartner.

Here is one example, and not an unusual one, of the many news flashes I've heard over the years:

Mommy and Daddy had a great big fight last night because Daddy drinks too much beer, but then they kissed and took a bath together to save water.

Teach respect for our National Anthem and the Pledge of Allegiance

Even though the concept behind both is difficult to grasp, insist on a reverent attitude during both. Standing still and placing your hand over your heart is enough at this age. Memorizing the words will come with repetition.

Do not tolerate rudeness.

It is normal for kindergartners to be egocentric, demanding attention on a whim. Reinforce good manners, especially when it comes to not interrupting others, a common bone of contention with elementary teachers. Demonstrate stellar behavior yourself and apologize when you catch yourself violating proper etiquette.

Teach good manners and polite responses.

Make these phrases a consistent part of your family's vocabulary.

- Please.
- May I?
- Thank you.
- Excuse me.
- I'm sorry.
- You first.
- I apologize for interrupting.
- May I be excused?

(Suggested reading: *Manners Can Be Fun* by Munro Leaf; *Dear Miss Perfect: A Beast's Guide to Proper Behavior* by Sandra Dutton; or *Please! Thank You! A Mind Your Manners! Storybook* by Jillian Harker which includes some reward stickers; and *The Berenstain Bears Forget Their Manners*, by Stan Berenstain and Jan Berenstain.)

Be vigilant about teaching good hygiene.

Besides raising a healthy, well turned out child, you'll help school employees control their gag reflexes. Focus on these things:

- Wash all crust and dust off daily.
- Brush your teeth.
- Wear clean clothes every day, including your underwear.
- Wipe out or wash your shoes when they smell.

> Use tissues, not fingers, to clean your nose.
> Wash hands before eating and after using the restroom.
> Sneeze and cough into the crook of your elbow.
> No spitting out food unless you quietly spit it into a napkin, holding the napkin close to your mouth so that no one can see the food. Fold the napkin to hide the food, and then throw it away.

(Suggested reading: *Germs are Not for Sharing* by Elizabeth Verdick.)

Project a positive attitude about your responsibilities.

It is important for children to be willing to do what is expected of them, even when unpleasant. Your attitude about chores and your job will set the tone, so fake a cheery smile if you have to. If children are willing to cooperate at home, they should be able to conform to the demands of school as well.

Sometimes I have to do things at work that I don't like, but everyone has to do things they do not like. If we could do whatever we wanted all the time, we wouldn't know when we were really happy. We would be bored silly because we wouldn't know when we were having fun.

Whatever you do, make it a priority to schedule physical playtime for the whole family.

Stop feeling guilty about not getting enough exercise. Think about the fun you could have riding bikes together, taking walks with intermittent races down the street, or playing games that wear you down so that you will all release your endorphins (your happy hormones) and sleep better.[25]

The Importance of Learning Bus Rules

Some students end up in the principal's office for misbehaving on the bus when their behavior is otherwise very good. It appears to me that the littlest offenders do not understand what is expected of them, or get into trouble simply because they are impressionable and will mimic the bad behavior of older students. If you are worried about what might be happening between home and school, request that someone in a position of authority review a bus tape or two. Most districts now have cameras on buses to protect themselves legally and for evidence in settling disputes.

Some bus drivers are more lax on rules than others, but if you use the following guidelines for encouraging exemplary behavior, you're sure to keep your child out of trouble and safe as well. A fantastic way to teach acceptable and safe behavior is to practice following bus rules in the car.

> ➤ Do not stand in the road when waiting on the bus. Stand at least five giant steps away from the curb.
> ➤ Do not walk towards the bus until it is completely stopped and the driver has opened the door.
> ➤ If you must cross the road when getting on or off the bus, always look both ways first and walk in front of the bus, never behind the bus. Don't cross the street until the bus lights are blinking. Walk five giant steps away from the front of the bus so you can see the bus driver and the bus driver can see you.
> ➤ Sit in your assigned seat.
> ➤ Always stay seated when the bus is moving.
> ➤ Never yell or make loud noises because you will bother the driver who is trying to keep you safe.

➢ Do not touch others or their things. If someone is touching you or your things, tell the bus driver.

➢ If another student tells you to "keep a secret" about something that happens on the bus, you should tell the bus driver. If you are scared, tell Mommy or Daddy, or your teacher.

➢ If you see someone doing something bad, and you are scared to tell the bus driver, then tell your teacher as soon as you get to your classroom.

➢ Do not put your things in the walking aisle. Keep them beside you or underneath the seat in front of you where you can keep an eye on them.

➢ Do not put anything, including your head or hands, outside the bus windows.

➢ Do not leave anything behind, including your trash.

➢ Do not eat or drink on the bus.

➢ Do not write on the bus seats or walls.

➢ Do not scratch or poke holes in the bus seats.

➢ Say hello and goodbye to the bus driver. He or she cares about you.

➢ You should always feel safe on the bus, and if you don't, you need to tell the bus driver, your teacher, or Mommy and Daddy.

Smart parents try to snag the bus driver's cell phone number on the first day.

Bus drivers normally carry a copy of the students' emergency medical forms with them, so you won't need to reciprocate. Having the bus driver's number will save precious time in case your child fails to return home after school. If that should happen and you can't reach the bus driver, call the school immediately. It is common to find a kindergartner asleep in a bus seat, on the wrong bus, or sitting in the office after dawdling too long or using the bathroom instead of going straight to the loading zone.

Review the following situations several times prior to the start of school:

What should you do if you get on the wrong bus?

Sometimes it happens when there are substitute bus drivers, different bus numbers because of a breakdown, or students aren't paying close attention and board a bus that is near their usual loading spot. Sometimes bullies think it is hilarious to misdirect younger children, and sometimes it happens when two little buddies decide it would be great fun to go home together. Bus drivers look out for "stowaways" because of the potential inconvenience for everyone involved, but occasionally some slip through undetected.

Coach your child to always talk to the driver if something doesn't feel right no matter what anyone else says. If caught early enough, the bus driver can radio the correct bus to hook up and make the switch.

What if your bus doesn't show up in the morning?

You need to decide, depending upon your individual circumstances, what you want to happen. If you make an arrangement with a stay-at-home neighbor to handle the situation, be sure you have a back up plan in case that person isn't home on that particular day.

What if someone stops and offers you a ride?

Make this topic part of your "stranger danger" talk. (*Never accept a ride from anyone you don't know.*) To lessen the trauma of discovering that there might be some pretty scary people out there, read an appropriate children's book on the subject, preferably anytime other than bedtime.

(Suggested reading: *The Berenstain Bears Learn about Strangers* by Stan Berenstain and Jan Berenstain.)

What if you miss the bus that brings you home?

Go back inside the school and stay there. Look for an adult who will help you.

(Suggested reading: *Staying Safe on the Bus* by Joanne Mattern, and just for fun, read *Don't Let the Pigeon Drive the Bus!* by Mo Williems.)

Staying Out of Trouble in the Cafeteria

Many schools schedule recess immediately following lunch time. I'm betting that you can remember a few classmates who had to stay inside for wreaking havoc in the cafeteria. Practice good manners and a few simple rules at home for added insurance that your little one will be running for the playground on a regular basis.

➢ Remain in your seat until excused.
➢ Do not sit on your feet or stand on your knees. Sit with your legs in front of you and your feet on the floor (or hanging down).
➢ Eat a few bites of everything, even if you do not like the taste, or even if you are not hungry. (Some teachers will insist upon it and some won't, but it's a good idea anyway.)
➢ Do not spit out food. If you have to because you feel something strange when you bite down (such as a loose tooth!), or you have taken too big a bite and you're afraid you'll choke, then spit it into a napkin and fold it up to throw it away.
➢ If you are choking, don't wait for help. Get up and run to the nearest adult! Put your hand on your throat if no one understands what is wrong.
➢ Don't share food. (This will keep beggars and germs at bay.)
➢ Be careful not to spill your drink. Always grab it with both hands and drink every drop so you won't end up wearing it.
➢ Use your napkin to wipe your face and hands. Do not rub your hands on your clothes, on the table, or on the seat to clean them off.
➢ No yelling or loud talking.
➢ Keep your hands to yourself. Do not touch others or their food.

➢ If you drop food on the floor, pick it up with a napkin and throw it away. Do not eat anything that has been on the floor.

➢ If you drop your spoon or fork on the floor, pick it up, but do not use it. Raise your hand and ask for a clean one. Don't forget to say *please.*

➢ Pick up all your trash and throw it away.

➢ Be careful not to throw away your spoon or fork, bowls, or containers that can be washed and used again. (You may have to use disposable items in a packed lunch until your child is mature enough to know the difference.)

➢ Carry your plate/tray with both hands and keep it flat so you won't spill any left over food.

➢ Always say *thank you* to the cooks and the people who help you.

How Do You Know if Your Child is Too Sick to Go to School?

First, let's briefly review what I mentioned in the registration section about medications. Remember that no child is ever permitted to self-medicate, so if you do not know the policies for sending medications to school, call the school nurse. If you are permitted to send them with your child, find out if they must be sent in the original pill bottles. If so, be sure to copy all the information off of the label beforehand to follow at home. Additionally, you would be wise to send the over-the-counter medications that your child best responds to so it can be housed in the nurse's station. (Put your child's name on the bottle.) Sometimes kids can bounce back and stay at school after a dose of something and a few minutes of rest.

Seriously ill or injured children may qualify for a certified tutor to come to your home. Unless your child has special educational needs, you and/or your caregiver should be able to monitor the work to be done yourselves. In the event that you would need a tutor, you will be required to have your doctor fill out a form provided by the school.

The following information is typical, or "average," of the guidelines that most schools follow; however, it should never supersede the advice of your pediatrician.[26]

Colds

Coughing and/or a runny nose is okay, but don't send your child with a fever of 100 degrees or more for at least 24 hours after it breaks.[27]

Vomiting or Diarrhea

Opinions may vary, but a safe bet is to wait until two meals have been properly digested before returning to school.

Conjunctivitis (Pink Eye)

Even though several things can cause redness, pain, swelling, or a discharge from the eye, the school nurse may insist that you seek medical attention immediately. This bacterial infection is highly contagious and that is why children are not permitted to return to school until cleared by a physician.[28] Your entire family should be vigilant about hand washing and cleaning with anti-bacterial products to completely break the cycle.

Strep Throat

Some of the signs are a fever, difficulty swallowing, listlessness, sore-looking redness in the back of the throat and/or a scummy white coating on the tongue. It is contagious, so you'll need doctor clearance before returning to school.[29]

Ear Infection

See the doctor immediately at the onset of symptoms. Once the pain has subsided, your child is good to go unless listless or dizzy.[30] (For temporary relief, aim the warm air from a blow dryer into the ear canal. Hold your free hand near the ear to be certain you are not burning the earlobe.)

Chicken Pox

All scabs must be completely dry before returning to school. Even after receiving the vaccine, there is still a chance of contracting this illness, but the duration and symptoms will be mild compared to those of non-vaccinated children.[31]

Injuries

Crutches and wheelchairs are not the hindrance they used to be now that schools are required to be handicapped accessible. If you are worried about boisterous hallway traffic, loose balls on the playground, or anything else that might jeopardize healing, talk to the school nurse and/or the teacher. They should be able to reassure you that extra precautions will be taken to prevent mishaps.

(Suggested reading for parents: *Boost Your Child's Immune System: A Program and Recipes for Raising Strong, Healthy Kids* by Lucy Burney.)

Lice: Everyone's Friend

Once school begins and you see your kid scratching his or her noggin, don't make the mistake of just assuming you're raising a deep thinker. The most non-prejudiced critters on earth are lice. They do not discriminate against race, religion, or social status; they love to feed on the blood of anyone and everyone. If these creatures happen to invade your home, however, there is no need to call in the National Guard or burn your house to the ground.

Pediculosis capitis, better known as head lice or "cooties," can infest anyone no matter how clean. In fact, they actually prefer squeaky clean hair.[32] They are wingless, but are speedy little devils, and crawl from head to head during a quick hug or accidental head bang. They are the reason why we preach in schools not to share combs, brushes, or hats. They are the reason why we tell you to keep long hair braided or pulled into a nice tight ponytail. They are the reason why you should cancel all sleepovers when you are alerted that these pesky varmints have been detected in your child's vicinity.

The school nurse will periodically launch an all-out search to be sure that if the problem exists, it will be isolated as soon as possible. Unfortunately, parents of infested children are often shocked and upset when they find out that "isolating the problem" means exclusion from school. If this happens to you, take immediate action.

If you receive a call to pick up your child, don't leave without books and materials to keep up with assignments.

If you are like most parents, you will initially be mortified. If it happens to you, just remember that more children contract lice than all the other childhood diseases combined.[33] It is normal to feel embarrassed, even though you shouldn't, especially when you talk to the teacher about how you'll communicate about homework until cleared to return to school. Teachers are well aware of how easy it is to pick up, they probably know of at least one staff member who has had it, and they are fully aware that they are not immune to it either.

What do you do first?

Be sure to ask the school nurse for the most recent information available about treatments and then head for the drug store. Pharmaceutical companies are continuously working to develop products that work faster, with less toxicity, and less mess, so hopefully if you ever need a cure, something miraculous will be available.If nothing else is available, look for the newest products on the market that have been specifically developed to kill lice that have become resistant to older remedies. (LiceMD is great for thick or tangly hair!)

It is important that you get rid of every last nit so you won't be forced into a repeat performance. Look for a kit that comes with a metal comb, rather than cheap plastic. The metal will be much more aggressive in removing both live bugs and their eggs, called "nits."

What about home remedies?

Home remedies such as mayonnaise, Vaseline, butter, or olive oil may work, but products developed specifically for lice removal are much less messy and easier to get out of your hair. If you can't get to a store, I'd use these things as a last resort. Whatever you do, do *not* use pesticides or harsh chemicals on the scalp. They are not only health hazards, most are also flammable. If you are desperate, or insist on using a home remedy anyway, olive oil is the least smelly and the easiest to wash out.

(1) Coat hair with olive oil and wrap with plastic wrap.
(2) Wait two hours, then shampoo.
(3) Rinse out shampoo with water.
(4) Rinse hair with white vinegar.
(5) Use water as a final rinse.
(6) Comb with a fine toothed comb, concentrating on removing nits attached to hair shafts.[34]

If the thought of using any home remedy grosses you out, and you are leery of the harsh chemicals in lice shampoos, you can also try using Cetaphil, a cleanser meant to fight acne. The jury is still out, but some parents swear by it. It was originally discovered by someone who subsequently tried to market it illegally under another name and was caught.[35]

(1) Coat the hair with Cetaphil cleanser.

(2) Blow the hair dry until "slightly crusty."
(3) Leave on for 8 hours.
(4) Wash hair with regular shampoo.
(5) Comb with a fine toothed comb, concentrating on removing nits attached to hair shafts.[36]

What are you looking for?

The actual insect is very tiny and hard to spot. Be forewarned that using a bright light during your search will cause them to scamper away to another part of the scalp. The trick is to look closely the second you lift a section of hair. Using a magnifying glass may help.

If you are having trouble spotting them, pay particular attention to the nape of the neck and around the ears where they are most likely to congregate. If you are lucky enough to grab one, stick it on a piece of tape so it won't get away. It is imperative that you dispose of them, as well as the nits, in a sealed plastic bag. At the end of the "chase," make sure you scrub underneath your fingernails because they can temporarily survive there as well.

Red blotches are also evidence of their presence as they survive by feeding on the blood of the victim's scalp. Contrary to popular belief, they may not itch at first, unless you are allergic to the bugs. That's why some people are unaware of their presence until two or three months later when an itching sensation finally occurs.[37]

Nits are much easier to see because they are attached to hair strands. They are also tiny, and when first laid, appear anywhere from a yellow to grayish-white color. As they age, they take on a brownish tint. You will know if you are looking at a nit, as opposed to merely a flake of dandruff or residue from hair products, when you try to remove it. Nits cannot be plucked off with your fingers or washed away with regular shampoo. In fact, the worst thing you can do is use any kind of cream rinse or hair conditioner because, and pardon the pun; it will "egg" them on by protecting them.[38]

If you are having trouble eliminating the problem, or if you spot severe rashes or sores, call your pediatrician. There are oral therapies available that must be prescribed by a doctor.

Now for the really bad news...

You're going to need to clean your house and the inside of your vehicle. Experts have widely differing opinions on the length of time that lice can exist without feeding off of human blood; anywhere from 50 hours to three weeks. Even if you can abandon your quarters and vehicle for whatever length of time is needed, you'll still want to eradicate all the dead carcasses. Here's an itemized list of chores for you:

> ➤ Wash all bedding every night until all nits are completely gone from the scalp.
> ➤ Wash all clothing the same day it is worn and keep it in a tied garbage bag until it hits the washing machine.
> ➤ Put everything you can in a hot dryer for 20 minutes and the heat will kill lice and nits as well.
> ➤ Soak all combs, brushes, barrettes, and other hair accessories in hot water for at least 10 minutes or put them in your dishwasher. You may also soak them in rubbing alcohol.
> ➤ Vacuum upholstery, carpets, stuffed animals, etc.
> ➤ Whatever cannot be washed or vacuumed should be placed in plastic garbage bags. (Researchers operating on behalf of the National Pediculosis Association concluded in 2006 that if lice cannot return to a human head within 50-60 hours, they will die.[39])
> ➤ Do not worry about pets. They are not carriers.
> ➤ Think about what may have been contaminated. Don't forget about things like the foam padding on bicycle or batting helmets.
> ➤ Lastly, examine everyone who lives in your household, and have someone check your head as well.

When can your child return to school?

When you can no longer find any evidence of bugs or nits, you're back in as long as the nurse doesn't find any either. She will have to verify that your child's scalp is clear because just one nit will hatch in 7–10 days and spread the joy all over again.

And finally, why wait for the school to make the gruesome discovery?

Make periodic checks to prevent having to go through this misery in the first place. It is unlikely that having lice will cause any social stigma for a child during the first few years of school, but later on, it could be devastating. You can best explain the causes and prevent a snooty attitude about it by utilizing one of the following children's books: *There's a Louse in my House* by Cheri Hayes, *Yikes-Lice* by Donna Cafey, or *Scritch Scratch* by Marium Moss.

Dealing with a Child Who Doesn't Want to Go to School

The younger the child, the more likely you'll have to deal with "separation anxiety." Starting school is when the payoff may come for having taken the time to arrange playdates and activities away from home and away from you. Another dose of preventative medicine would be to hire a trustworthy babysitter, friend, or relative to take your child to the school playground during off hours.

Children who are part of a stable family unit in which their parents take the time to take care of their relationship also feel more secure away from home. Showing affection and playfulness with one another will help reinforce this feeling.

Nevertheless, if you have made the conscious decision that it is time to start school, then the most critical moment you must plan for is the first day of school. Prior to that day, you must always vow to talk positively about every single thing that has anything to do with going to school. Do NOT say:

You have to start school this year.

However you choose to approach it, make it sound like a new adventure, not a prison sentence. Address the subject with the same enthusiasm you would have if you were planning a trip to Disney World.

Whoo hoo! You get to go to school this year, you lucky dog! I wish I could go to school again.

Try not to appear nervous or worried. Act as if you have no doubt in your mind that your child will love it. As soon as you begin talking about going to school, toot your horn every time you drive by and say, "There's your school!" Children take their emotional cues from the adults they depend on. Be reassuring that teachers are trustworthy people and work in schools because they love children. Talk fondly about the teachers you had and how they took good care of you.

When the big day finally comes, you must keep smiling and remain upbeat. When it's time to finally let go of that little hand, don't hesitate for even a second. Quickly hug and kiss your child goodbye, and then vamoose.

Do not linger no matter what. If you do, you will be sending a very bad message—one that says:

If you cry and carry on, then I'll stay. The longer I stay, the weaker I will get and maybe, just maybe, you won't have to go after all.

Don't ever say or do anything that makes going to school seem like it might be an optional activity. Don't say how awful it will be for you too, and how much you'll miss him or her. Once your child figures out that you are sensitive to a display of distress, you will be in big trouble. If you buckle to the pressure of whining and crying for even one day, you'll just set yourself up for more of the same.

Some anxiety may be the fear of not knowing exactly where he or she is going once there. To be certain that this isn't the case, visit the school ahead of time and trace the path from the point of arrival to the classroom. Most teachers spend days and even weeks preparing for opening day, so purchase or prepare a small treat to drop off when you stop by. Don't visit longer than a few minutes because he or she will have lots to do!

You can make school seem like a friendly place by attending school carnivals, open houses, ball games, concerts, and other activities that are open to the public in the years prior to starting school. If permissible, you may also make periodic trips to the playground.

Remain positive and steadfast when it comes to school attendance, and remember:

Facing what you fear is the best way to build self-confidence.

(Suggested reading: *The Kissing Hand* by Audrey Penn.)

Buy a reliable thermometer.

Children at this age quickly make the association between being sick and staying home. You can play and win the same game the school nurse plays with children who are "frequent flyers"—in and out of the school clinic—by using a thermometer. First, pretend to take the claim seriously: *You're sick? We'd better take your temperature.* And when there's no temperature, you say, *That's too bad. You're going to have to go to school.*

What if your child throws up?

Some children become so upset and cry so hard that their irregular breathing causes them to upchuck. This emotionally induced vomiting, called "psychogenic vomiting," is more common than you might think.[40] A clever child will figure out the physical mechanics and purposely bring on an attack to manipulate you.

Similarly, some children will figure out that if they pick their noses long and/or deep enough, they can draw blood. The fancy name for this disgusting self-abuse is called "digital trauma."[41]

The cure for school phobia is simple.

Some children develop "school phobia," a recognized psychological condition in which they may or may not exhibit physical symptoms such as headaches, upset stomach, diarrhea, and even dizziness.[42] Even if a doctor makes such a diagnosis, the best cure is to get right back into the saddle. The longer he or she stays home, the harder it will be to return to school.

Whether the symptoms seem real or imagined, be sympathetic, but express your concern all the way to the bus stop or to the front door of the school. The longer your child stays home, the farther he or she will fall behind academically, which will only increase the level of anxiety upon returning to school. While absent, other children will have been networking and establishing friendships which will further compound the problem.

If you still think you can't muster up the guts to stand firm, try this visualization exercise:

Imagine your precious angel at age thirty, still living with you, uneducated, and whining about having to look for a job.

Your attitude about missing school will create a blueprint that will inevitably carry over into adulthood. Even when we don't feel 100 percent some days, we have to tough it out. Kids will benefit in the long run from doing the same.

If you adhere to a few "old school" rules, borrowed from my parents, you should be able to keep this problem in check for the next 13 years.

- ➤ If you don't go to school, you stay in bed all day.
- ➤ If you feel better before noon, you will go back to school.
- ➤ If you don't go to school, you can't go out of the house for the rest of the day.
- ➤ If you don't go to school on Friday, you can't go anywhere all weekend except for church.
- ➤ You cannot have company, with the exception of a classmate dropping off makeup work.
- ➤ If you don't go to school, no one can come over to play.

If these tactics fail to deter an alleged "faker," then call his or her bluff. Say, *You are going to school anyway, and if you don't feel better after a while, ask to see the school nurse.* Then call and clue her in. She'll not only know how to handle it, she probably won't even have to try. Most kids are okay once they arrive, and besides, I can assure you that no one will allow your child to spend the day slumped over a desk.

Read the time-honored tale of *The Boy Who Cried Wolf* over and over to a hypochondriac.

It is one of Aesop's fables that has been tweaked and reprinted several times, but the basic message is always the same: *If you continuously lie about something, no one will believe you when you are telling the truth.*

What if your child is screaming, crying, and thrashing around?

It is discouraging for us to find out that the root of a truancy problem is a parent's reluctance to drag a child to school and face the embarrassment of an all-out tantrum. If this is your story, then I've got some really good news for you. We actually prefer that you breeze in, hand over the goods, and then scram. It is surprising how fast most children will calm down and drop the theatrics once it is clear that they have been left behind. If you cannot stomach such a scene, then find an adult who is willing to "make the drop" for you.

Your child may never be one of those "tra-la-la-I'm-off-to-school-kids," but insisting on regular attendance is a whole lot easier than going to court and facing a judge on a truancy charge.

Don't be discouraged or surprised by any backsliding.

You may need to re-address this problem after long weekends, holidays, or after any unsettling events. Just stay the course. Never give in. No negotiating. Period.

What to Do about a Kid Who Won't Get Out of Bed

If you can initiate a pretty good giggling fit, you might be able to cajole your little sleepyhead out of bed. Get out your feather duster and pretend to be dusting the bedroom, but don't forget to concentrate on those little ears and nose. Set alarm clocks all around the bed and then watch the fun from the doorway. Get out your trumpet from high school and play revelry. Blast some loud music with a great beat and dance on the bed. Snuggle up close and pretend to snore like a gorilla. Stir up the family dog and hide its toys under the covers. Just do whatever works.

If teasing is not your style, you might experiment with my mother's no-fail method. She could snap me out of a stupor by handing me a "wake-up wash cloth," which was nice and warm. After wiping my face, I really did feel much better about having to get up, especially if I knew my dad was on his way up the stairs.

If nothing seems to work, you may have to resort to some good old-fashioned man-handling. Yank off those covers and drag your Rumpelstiltskin, screaming or not, out of bed.

On a more serious note, lack of sleep impairs the ability to retain what is learned and weakens problem solving skills, but being tired isn't a valid reason for missing school. Unless a child is recovering from an illness, or an unavoidable family event has interrupted a regular sleep cycle, don't cave in to any whining. If you do not agree that tiredness is not a valid excuse, then ask yourself this:

Do you have to go to work when you are tired? Do you have to cook, clean, mow, pay bills, run errands, etc., when you are pooped?

Sure you do. My point being that sending a sleepy child to school might seem cruel, but in the long run, that child will learn to tough out a hard day, just like you.

If this is only an occasional occurrence then you're doing great as a parent. If it is an ongoing problem then try these strategies to cure your lethargic grump:

> ➢ Keep backing up his or her bedtime until you get it right. Having to rouse your child more than once is a bad sign. Children's needs vary, but most kindergartners need at least 10 to 12 hours per night.

> ➢ Stick to a routine such as putting on pajamas, brushing teeth, saying prayers, reading a bedtime story, and then ending it all with a final goodnight kiss. Do the same thing every night in exactly the same order. Bedtime rituals signal the body that it's time to go to sleep, plus you'll eliminate power struggles because there will be no question about "what comes next."

> ➢ Soften your voice and stop all lecturing a couple of hours before you begin your bedtime routine. It will alleviate stressful feelings, especially if you've had a rocky evening together, and your child will feel loved.

> ➢ Cut out all physical activity a couple of hours before bedtime.

> ➢ Monitor TV shows. What may seem mild to you can conger up images of monsters, not just under the bed, but ones that we all fear who disguise themselves as human beings.

> ➢ Keep track of evening snacks and their effect on alertness. You may be able to avoid bedtime struggles just by eliminating common culprits such as sugary and/or caffeinated soft drinks.[43]

> ➢ Limit drinks to prevent nighttime visits to the bathroom.

> ➢ Don't forget how good a backrub can feel.

> ➢ You may be able to pinpoint the cause of sleeplessness and/or nighttime restlessness if you pray together. Afterwards, you can add your two cents to quell any fears. If the possibility of monsters in the closet or under the bed seems to be a sleep deterrent, create your own "anti-monster spray" by using a bottle of Fabreeze, or even just water in an empty spray bottle, to eradicate them before turning out the lights.

> ➢ Encourage a routine upon rising. Sometimes operating on "automatic pilot" will keep things moving along, i.e., *Go to the bathroom, wash your face, get dressed, comb your hair, eat breakfast...*

> ➢ Make your house feel "awake" in the morning. You can turn on the radio, initiate a conversation about something positive, eat breakfast

together, whatever—just greet the morning with a positive attitude. It will be infectious.

And finally, ask yourself one last question:

Is this the only attention I'm giving my child?

If this is a distinct possibility, then it is ultra-important that you spend more recreational, non-judgmental, giggling time together.

Taking the blame for a tardy child does not relieve you of your responsibility as a parent.

Telling the teacher or the office staff that it's your fault won't cut it. Tardy is tardy, no matter what the reason. Eventually you'll be reported to your local children's services agency or to juvenile court. Why would we make such a big deal out of being tardy?

A student who walks in 20 minutes late every day misses approximately 60 hours of school per year which adds up to a week and a half! Other students are also affected as they are distracted by a late arrival and cheated out of the time that the teacher must take to readjust the lunch count and attendance report, as well as taking the time to help get a late arrival on task.

Remember that teachers are human and can't help but feel irritated by chronic tardiness. They don't want to hear excuses; they just want everyone to arrive on time.

(Suggested reading: *The Going to Bed Book* by Saundra Boynton. It is a short and delightful tale about an ark full of animals preparing for bed. *Good Night Moon*, by Margaret Wise Brown, is also a good book for kids who tend to stall around at bedtime. If you want to inject some humor into the situation, read *Get Out of Bed!* by Robert Munsch, or *Don't Let the Pigeon Stay Up Late!* by Mo Willems.)

Excuses, Excuses, Excuses

"Sadie," a former student of mine, stopped by my office wanting advice about possibly changing careers. It didn't take much effort for me to be able to read between the lines. I could tell that she wasn't happy because her current employer expected her to do something that she just couldn't hack. It was something that she wasn't able to do when she was a student either, but it wasn't really her fault. Her parents were mostly to blame because they failed to teach her that becoming successful starts with an oh-so-simple, but necessary thing: *showing up*.

Sadly, Sadie had spent her childhood under the microscope of irrationally devoted parents who believed that a restless night's sleep, a skinned knee, or the trauma of seeing a dead possum along side the road were justification for staying home from school. She exemplifies the typical "over-parented" child who has failed to learn the importance of responsibility and commitment. Remember what happened to her when you're tempted to become lax about school attendance. Your attitude may very well become a blueprint that carries over into adulthood.

Use the following suggestions to guide you when it becomes necessary to miss school for reasons other than illness.

Doctor and Dentist Appointments

Try to schedule routine visits after school hours or during school holidays. If you can't, then try to coordinate appointments all on the same day. For other illnesses and problems that crop up, we realize, of course, that it is a necessary absence.

Family Vacations

We are well aware that some places of employment dictate vacation time. If there is no other way to take a family vacation without interrupting the school year, then make sure you do the following:

➤ Don't just take off. Explain your situation to the principal first.

➤ Tell the teacher at least a month in advance so that he or she can put together work for you to complete.

➤ Once you've received the work, start on it *before* your trip. The more you can do ahead of time, the more you'll be able to relax and enjoy your time together.

➤ Have everything completed and ready to turn in upon returning to school.

➤ Bring back something special to share with the teacher and class such as postcards or pictures.

The Death of a Relative or Close Friend

It is important for children to have a chance to grieve and learn about death through family members, especially if you hold tight to your religious beliefs and customs. The appropriate amount of time off should be based on your child's emotions, not your own feelings. Sometimes children are anxious to get back to school and regain a sense of normalcy. Resuming an interest in regular activities is a good sign.

If the death has seriously altered the family structure and/or raises the fear of further abandonment, enlist the help and support of the school counselor. Clingy behavior is one telltale sign that you might need assistance upon returning to school. The counselor can alert everyone from the secretaries to the principal to be ready with extra attention and support.

Family Emergencies

Please feel free to call the school and whine when something catastrophic happens to your family. If the secretaries are too busy to listen to you, ask for the guidance counselor, principal, or nurse. Knowledge about your situation is very important to us so that we will know how to comfort and help your child upon returning to school.

If you are dealing with the aftermath of a fire, flood, serious illness, car accident, etc., we may also be able to help you find resources, such as clothing, to assist with your family's recovery. Returning to a normal school routine can be very comforting in that it is one thing that will stay constant when the rest of the world seems turned up-side-down.

Observing Religious Holidays not Regularly Recognized by the District

Notify the teacher well in advance, especially if it means missing more than a day of instruction. You may be able to squeeze in makeup work ahead of time which will make the return to school much easier.

Moving

Hopefully you'll never have to deal with the upheaval of changing schools. If it has to happen, don't milk it or project the idea that the time out of school is a vacation. Every day missed is a lost opportunity to learn something. Let the school you're leaving know ahead of time so they can properly prepare records to send to ensure a smooth transition without any delays. Don't forget to return library books and settle up any fees owed before you leave.

Notify the new school that you'll be coming. They may be able to provide you with enrollment papers before you've actually moved. Make sure you have all the essential documents ready when you walk through the front door—birth certificate, custody papers, social security card, shot record, and proof of residency—as well as all the other information as outlined in the section entitled *Registration Papers*. Make sure you also jot down the address, phone number, and fax number of the school you are leaving.

The Ultimate Parental Sin

You want an excuse to miss work, so you keep your kid home from school under the pretense that he or she is "sick."

Whew. This is a bad idea for several reasons. Let's review those.

> ➤ This is an unnecessary day of missed instruction, and every absence creates a gap in learning.
> ➤ Your child will learn not to believe everything you say.
> ➤ This sends a message that it is okay to lie if we don't feel like doing something.
> ➤ Every absence, whether excused or not, becomes part of a student's permanent record.
> ➤ Kindergartners do not have much of a conversation filter and will, without a doubt, announce upon returning to school why they were absent. *My mom called her boss and said I was sick but I really wasn't.* If this is the case, then the teacher will no longer trust you, and will more than likely be irritated at the thought of having to put together makeup work for your frivolous day off.
> ➤ Even if you think you are raising an intellectual prodigy, missing school will cause some "disconnected learning" which prevents students from reaching their maximum potential.

Food for Thought

Let's start with breakfast. Kids need to eat a combination of foods to get their engines running, ingest nutrients to stay healthy, and stave off hunger until lunch time. Hearty, protein-rich foods such as eggs, bacon, sausage, and cheese, will stick to your ribs, but can cause sluggishness if served alone. When combined with carbohydrates, such as juice, milk, waffles, fruit, toast, and cereal, you'll provide the added fuel needed for energy and alertness. If you make sure that the combination includes some fiber—whole wheat bread, wheat cereal, oatmeal, citrus fruit, or strawberries—it will help sustain alertness until lunchtime as it slows "gastric emptying."[44]

Keep an eye on how specific foods may be affecting behavior, including snacks. Children metabolize food differently so don't rely solely on what you read and hear. You should aim for food combinations that result in being alert and in tune with activities without inducing hyperactivity.

What to do if your child won't eat breakfast.

Some kids aren't hungry when they first wake up. If this is the case, explore these options:

> Sometimes going to bed earlier will remedy the problem. Children who get enough sleep are generally more alert and raring to go.
> Shuffle your morning routine so that eating is the last thing done before leaving for school. Hunger may kick in by then.
> If you can work it out, make breakfast a regular event during which the entire family eats together so it is something to look forward to.
> Check and see if the school has a breakfast program. The cost will be minimal compared to lunch, and you'll be spared the mess at home.
> Try serving nontraditional breakfast food such as pizza. As long as it is nutritious, who cares?

> ➤ Make "fun to eat" foods. Use cookie cutters to dress up pancakes and toast. (You can eat the remnants.) Put food coloring in oatmeal or Cream of Wheat. You can even make "green eggs and ham" by scrambling the eggs with a little green food coloring.
> ➤ Keep "to go" foods such as bananas and cereal bars handy that can be eaten on the way to school in case hunger sets in at the last minute.

(Suggested reading: *Green Eggs and Ham* by Dr. Seuss, and *Elmo's Breakfast Bingo* by Random House.)

Would you like to save money and promote healthy eating for all your family members?

If so, mass packing could be the answer. It is just as easy to pack one lunch as two or more, so you may even be able to bow out of this chore as long as you can learn not to freak out about the mess. Most kindergartners would love to run the show if you'd let them, and who wouldn't be touched by a lunch lovingly packed by a child? (Your colleagues may be wildly entertained as well by what ends up on your menu.) Shop for healthy choices, and then lay everything out on the table in the morning or the night before where everyone can put together a lunch of their own choosing.

Thinking Outside the Lunch Box

Long gone are the days of the boring old bologna sandwich, bag of chips, and cookies for desert. Even though that combination might not sound half bad, we all know that we need to try and make healthier choices than that, especially when it comes to lowering our fat intake and hitting a few more food groups. The trick is finding out what will actually be chewed and swallowed instead of flung into the trash can. Another benefit of allowing your child to help pack his or her own lunch is that I can assure you that whatever goes in the box will probably end up down the right hatch.

Sandwiches

I'm not sure what the attraction is but kids who normally eat like birds will scarf down sandwiches even if made with whole grain or whole wheat bread if you trim off the crusts. You can also try smashing down the whole thing with a rolling pin, and/or using cookie cutters to make delectable looking shapes.

If you are raising a bread hater, be creative. Shop for alternatives to bread such as tortilla roll-ups, pita pockets, or bagels. You can also try toasting a couple of frozen waffles and smearing some peanut butter in between.

Fruit

Bananas are probably the easiest as far as preparation, even though some of my nurse friends are now telling me you're supposed to rinse off them off (leaving the peels on) when you unpack your groceries. Apples are also easy unless you have a picky eater who wants them pre-sliced. If so, buy one of those inexpensive contraptions that you smash down over the apple to slice it in one swoop. To keep the slices from turning brown, dip them in 7-Up or lemon juice. Or, you can skip dipping the slices to keep them fresh and just sprinkle them with cinnamon for an "apple pie" taste.

If you want to convert an anti-fruit eater, buy some caramel ice cream topping and drizzle it over the apple slices for a "caramel apple" treat.

Strawberries are usually expensive, but if you're going to do the mass packing thing, kids will only eat a few so you and your spouse can hog the rest.

If you are going to send something in the orange category, be sure to peel it, or at least slice it into quarters. Otherwise, you may as well go ahead and throw it in the trash. No one feels like peeling an orange and getting all sticky at lunch time, especially when there are more interesting things to do, like watching the kid who gargles his milk while singing.

Grapes are usually a hit, but you'll need to rinse them and put them in a bag or container.

Dried fruit and raisins can be bought pre-packaged, or to save money, buy them in bulk without added sugar, and bag them yourself.

Prepackaged apple sauce and fruit cups have always been popular and easy to pack, and companies are now adding new fruits to both lines such as strawberries, blueberries, and peaches.

Don't fall for the "fruit snack" scam at the grocery store. Most of them are nothing but sugar and starch with just a smidge of real fruit juice, so only count them as a desert.

If your child won't eat fruit without "dip," a healthy alternative to buying the sweetened type that comes ready made in containers is to pack flavored yogurt which can also be finished off with a spoon.

Nuts

They are a tremendous source of protein and various vitamins and minerals, depending upon which kind you buy. Look for them in bulk and bag them up yourself or buy them prepackaged for convenience.

High Energy Trail Mix

The best kind is homemade because you can tailor it to your individual taste. The basic recipe calls for raisins, peanuts, and M&M's, and then you can add other healthy foods. Some popular choices are dried fruits such as dates, apricots, apple chips, and banana chips; nuts such as almonds and hazelnuts; and sunflower seeds, granola and other healthy cereals.

Raw Veggies

Experiment at home to see which varieties will be eaten and which ones will end up being a waste of money. Cherry tomatoes, carrots, and celery seem to be the most popular, especially with a little dip. If you have a broccoli eater, you're in luck because this vegetable has the added bonus of containing calcium. Instead of trying to keep track of a small container, pour a little salad dressing in a snack-sized sealable bag.

A popular kid's recipe, "Ants on a Log," provides a serving of vegetables, protein, and fruit when you press raisins into celery sticks filled with peanut butter. You can also fill celery, sweet or green peppers, or tomatoes with cheese or sandwich spreads.

Shish-Ka-Bobs Without the Sticks

Cut up cheese, meat, veggies, or fruit into chunks and put them in sealable bags or containers.

Baked Chips

The new wave in health consciousness has forced major chip suppliers to offer something that isn't fried in a vat of oil, so baked varieties are now easy to find. Tortilla chips can be dipped in chunky salsa for a serving of vegetables.

Frozen Bottled Water

I can't emphasize enough what a great idea this is for a lunchtime beverage. If it gets knocked over, who cares? It doesn't stain, doesn't cause cavities, doesn't contain empty calories, and it's easy to pack. I'd say it's cheap too, but that depends upon how many empty bottles make it home for you to refill and use again. Don't forget to twist new bottles open and closed to break the initial seal before packing so it will be easier for little hands to manage.

Other Drinks

There is no law that says you have to provide milk at every meal. You can provide calcium by packing cheese, cottage cheese, yogurt, or even broccoli. If you decide to send money for milk along with a packed lunch, find out what kind of hassle this involves. Sometimes kids have to wait in the regular lunch line just to get a container of milk, and some students never drink it anyway if it is too difficult to get open.

There are all kinds of juice drinks that you can send, but again, there are many pitfalls. They can also be hard to open, especially if they have one of those attached straws that you're supposed to poke through a specially marked hole. The ones that are bad for you can be chock-full of added sugar and empty calories, and many of the 100 percent juice brands contain sorbitol which can sometimes cause diarrhea in children.[45] The expense, the inconvenience, and the mess just aren't worth it, so again I recommend aiming for natural hydration with a bottle of water.

Yogurt

You can send prepackaged, flavored containers, or you can buy plain or vanilla in bulk and make your own parfait by adding some fruit and/or granola. Layer the fruit on top of the yogurt, and then add the granola on top to keep it crunchy.

Snack Bars

Instead of regular candy bars, check out the variety of healthy protein and cereal bars now available. Compare labels to make sure you're getting the healthiest brands.

Salads

If you're lucky enough to be raising a salad eater, make a meal of it by adding the works: meat, cheese, raw veggies, croutons, nuts, and other toppings.

Whole Grain and Fiber Fortified Crackers

If you wimp out and buy the prepackaged kind, read the label to make sure they are not made out of cardboard. Otherwise, you should check out the new lines of crackers that are more nutritious than ever. Cheese or sandwich spreads can be dolloped into a Baggie or into a piece of foil and used as a "dip." You can also cut up lunch meat and cheese for little cracker sandwiches.

Cereal

You can bag up sweetened brands as a dessert, or put healthy brands in a sealed container and send money for a carton of milk.

Cottage Cheese

Add a little jam or jelly and see if that nose still turns up.

Hard Boiled Eggs

If you're raising a salt addict who won't eat an egg without it, shake a little into a sealable bag (or use a salt substitute) along with the egg.

Beef Wellington, Lobster Bisque, Roasted Pheasant, etc.

There are all kinds of contraptions out there that will keep food warm that you can fill with an entrée from the night before, or with a dish you make specifically to scoop up for lunches all week. The downside is that you'll have to microwave the food in the morning and then hope the dirty container makes it home so you can wash and reuse it. Please do not expect a school employee to microwave or help prepare anything. Our time is entirely too regimented to perform special favors.

Dessert

Let's be realistic. The more crappy, sweet stuff you pack, the less chance that anything healthy is going to be eaten, so don't over do it.

How will you know if you are wasting your money?

You won't know for sure what is being eaten and what is not, but you can look for clues. If your child seems to be starving after school even though his or her lunch box is empty, you might want to find out who supervises lunch time and ask him or her to investigate before you increase the amount of food you're sending. Some kids chat instead of eating and then dump everything in the trash. Some fall prey to beggars who find the lunch you've packed to be much more appetizing than what they have in front of them. And finally, some have trouble getting prepackaged foods open and are too shy to ask for help, and again, just toss everything, eaten or not, into the trash.

As long as your child is getting nutrients at home, continues to grow, and doesn't appear sickly, you shouldn't consider poor eating habits at school to be a crisis.

If you are constantly worried about poor eating habits, you might want to check out Jessica Seinfield's cookbook entitled *Deceptively Delicious*, or Missy Chase Lapine's *The Sneaky Chef: Simple Strategies for Hiding Healthy Foods in Kids' Favorite Meals.* They have found ways to sneak nutritious food into kid-friendly dishes, such as pureed carrots and spinach in brownies, cauliflower in scrambled eggs, and spinach in blueberry oatmeal bars. Best of all, their recipes are easy to prepare.

Check out policies about "delivering" food during lunch time before you show up unannounced.

Some schools do not allow fast food or pizza to be brought in by you, or anyone else. The reasons are varied, but usually sound. Food management in schools are generally non-profit but typically struggle to stay afloat financially. Administrators may support their efforts to get students to buy their food by banning anything other than a lunch brought from home. The extra traffic in and out of the school may also be viewed as too much of an interruption for staff in charge of monitoring visitors and potential security risks. And finally, you don't want to create more of a hassle for lunch room supervisors. If food isn't delivered on time, they have to deal with students who are not finished eating when it's time to leave the cafeteria.

A forgotten lunch or lunch money is another story. It happens all the time and we expect it. Just drop it off in the office.

(Suggested reading: *Eat Your Peas Louise* by Pegeen Snow, *Eating the Alphabet: Fruits and Vegetables from A to Z* by Lois Ehlert, and *Grover's Guide to Good Eating* by Naomi Kleinberg.)

Life is Fair in Kindergarten

Not really. Life is never fair, and you know it, but kindergarten teachers do their best to even the score for their students. You can help by cooperating in the following ways:

Don't send any special treats unless you send enough for the entire class.

And before you do, make sure you send a note ahead of time so that you will know if your timing is bad. I can assure you that Halloween and Christmas regularly elicit an avalanche of sweets, so try to avoid those holidays unless you've signed up to help with a classroom party.

Birthday treats are usually welcome, especially at the end of the school day when we can send your child home so you can enjoy the effects of the sugar high rather than us. Checking ahead will also enable the teacher to alert you to any food allergies. Even though the thought of sending an alternate treat that tastes like shoe leather does not appeal to you, remember that children on restricted diets are used to the taste.

If you want to be mentioned in the teachers' lounge in a favorable light, send individual treats in plastic bags or tied up in cellophane—not cake, ice cream, or anything that has to be divided up or "served." Think of the cleanup involved before you shop or bake, and remember that under no circumstances should you ever send candles to light.

If you are discouraged from sending any edible treats, you could send books, coloring books, colorful pencils, jump ropes, games, and other inexpensive toys that kids may enjoy.

Do not show up unannounced. Teachers follow a structured day that includes art, music, physical education, and recess during which students may not be in their regular classrooms.

And lastly, if you are kind enough to help clean up, do not seize the opportunity to initiate an impromptu parent-teacher conference. If the teacher has time and speaks up first, fantastic. Otherwise, keep quiet.

If you receive directions from the teacher on how to prepare for special events, don't shirk your duties as a parent or deviate from the plan.

If the teacher wants you to decorate a box for Valentine's Day and help your child fill out a card for every last student in the class, then do it. If you are supposed to plant seeds in an egg carton or fill out a family tree, don't you dare toss the directions in the trash. Whatever the teacher asks you to do, vow that you will do it with a cheerful attitude. The last thing you want to do is demonstrate bad behavior that may be mimicked by your own child, so do not whine or procrastinate. An uncooperative attitude may also undermine the authority of the teacher if you, the boss of his or her other universe, refuse to do as you are told.

On the flip side, don't decide that you "have a better idea," and then try to charm or bully the teacher into doing something that involves additional time, money, or confusion. If you want to be a professional party planner, please find another place to experiment.

Don't send party invitations to school.

It doesn't matter if you intend to invite the entire class or not, don't do it. Parents who don't know you may bug the teacher to try to find out if you are operating a meth lab in your basement. When invitations don't make it all the way home, the last thing school personnel have time for is finding out if a child had an invitation to begin with or just decided to invite him- or herself. Just don't do it. Teachers have enough hats to wear without being expected to also serve as the class social director.

Don't expect to be a full-time volunteer in your child's classroom.

There will be a lot of parents who are just as excited as you are about getting to spend time in their child's classroom so don't hog all the time slots. If you have that kind of time and energy you should volunteer to work anywhere in the building. Children need to develop a sense of independence, especially if "cutting the cord" has been a traumatic experience to begin with, so always being accessible is not a good idea. Besides, you don't want to take the fun out of your after-school conversations.

Make sure you do something to help out the Parent-Teacher Organization.

These organizations typically buy extra classroom materials and often provide memorable and worthwhile activities that schools normally can't afford. If popping popcorn for three hours straight at a school carnival isn't your bag, then you can donate baked goods, prizes, or money. If you are broke, donate your time to make signs, decorate, or even make the calls to recruit other volunteers.

If nothing else, participate in fund-raisers by peddling items to family members and friends who have done the same to you.

Do not expect special treatment of any kind.

If you want to stay out of the principal's office, make sure you pay attention during orientation and read all the handouts word for word. You are expected to follow rules and procedures just like everyone else.

No matter how friendly you become with school personnel, follow the procedures for signing in when entering the building. Don't ask if you can deliver homework or a packed lunch directly to the classroom. Leave forgotten items in the office to be picked up later. This isn't just a safety issue; teachers would rather not have their classes interrupted.

Reading—The Basis of Student Success

There is much more involved in learning to read than sitting down together and muddling your way, word by word, through a book. In fact, forcing your child to do such a thing will only make reading look like drudgery instead of the convenience and enjoyable pleasure that it should appear to be. Placing reading materials throughout your home is one way to help project that image. Keep books, magazines, and newspapers in the bathroom, on night stands, where people normally sit to watch TV, and even in the car.

There are a multitude of things you can do to encourage the development of reading fluency and comprehension in the everyday activities that you are already doing. There are also some very simple activities you can initiate that are fantastic precursors to learning to read. When you figure out which activities seem to be the most enjoyable for both of you, keep doing those things. Once you've developed a good little independent reader, you can use the time to sit together, but read separately. Hopefully you'll be able to rediscover the joy of reading for your own amusement, something that so many adults fail to take time for. Until that day, just be glad you're not working together on calculus homework.

It all starts with the alphabet.

If you are still practicing the basic sequence of the alphabet, then start singing. It's the easiest way to memorize the correct pronunciation of all the letters as long as you enunciate clearly. You can also easily find books, games, coloring books, and a host of toys that encourage letter recognition; otherwise, you can always rely on the old fashioned pencil and paper method.

Invest in a few sets of magnetic letters that you can slide around on your refrigerator. You can graduate from identifying letters to forming words and then move on to composing important messages such as, *I love you Daddy!* Here are some additional challenges to reach for as skills develop:

- ➤ Match up lower and upper case letters.
- ➤ Put lower or uppercase letters in the proper alphabetic sequence.
- ➤ Practice changing just one letter to make a new word, such as *me* and then *my.*
- ➤ Practice changing letters to make rhyming words, such as *sat, hat,* and *rat.*
- ➤ Practice putting the "menu" together.
- ➤ Sort the letters into colors, and then spell the color.
- ➤ Learn to spell the names of friends and family members. (This is great practice for using a mix of upper and lower case letters.)
- ➤ Identify vowels and spell a word using each sound.
- ➤ Make grocery list reminders.

(Suggested reading: *Chicka Chicka Boom Boom* by Bill Martin, Jr., and as with many books, if you perform a simple Internet search, you might find accompanying learning activities to go along with the story. I also recommend Brian P. Cleary's books: *Stop and Go, Yes, and No, What is an Antonym?; Pitch and Throw, Grasp and Know, What is a Synonym?;* and *How Much Can a Bare Bear Bear?, What are Homonyms and Homophones?*)

Phonemic awareness is also an important skill that needs to be developed before preparing to learn to read.[46]

Phonemic awareness is the ability to "hear" the sounds that are put together to make up a word. *What sounds do you hear in the word "cat?"* (*K-a-t.*) Being able to identify individual sounds enables young readers to learn how to sound out words much faster when they start analyzing them in print.

Learning to Read Shouldn't Feed Like Work

Pushing too hard or too early may turn your child off completely. Take it easy before kindergarten and provide opportunities to learn to love the magic of language and books.

- ➤ Read to your child everyday, even if it is only a bedtime story.
- ➤ Run a finger under the words as you read. This will demonstrate how we read from top to bottom and left to right.
- ➤ Purchase a few books that have accompanying recordings, and exercise patience when you've heard the same stories for the

umpteenth time. Keep a couple of books and recordings in the car. (Suggested reading: *Is Your Mama a Llama?* by Deborah Guarino. The recording has a mambo-like background beat.)

➢ Make your own recordings for babysitters to play at bedtime, or just for the comforting feeling of hearing an absent parent's voice.

➢ Get a library card and browse the bookshelves together.

➢ Attend programs meant to entertain children at bookstores and libraries.

➢ Look for free interactive, age-appropriate reading materials online. (Don't waste money on software that will be mastered quickly.) Many websites are designed to highlight words as they are read to your child. (Suggestions: www.internet4classrooms.com and www.starfall.com)

➢ Have fun with words. *Can you think of any words that rhyme with your name? Can you think of any words that start with the same sound? Let's see who can think of the most words that start with the same letter.*

➢ When you are out and about, point out signs and "read" them. Words such as "stop" and "Red Lobster" will be associated with colors and shapes, but you can turn them into instantly recognizable "sight words" if you reinforce them by printing them on plain paper at home.

➢ Demonstrate how you use a phone book to order a pizza, how you use a newspaper to see what is playing at the movies, and how to check the directions on a box of brownie mix to see what other ingredients you need to buy, etc.

➢ When looking for a treat or a toy, "decode" the outside label. Say, *If you want microwave popcorn that has butter in it, we need to look for the word "butter" on the package. It begins with a "b." Do you see any words that begin with "b"?*

➢ You can "label" objects around the house with note cards, and then discard them as words become familiar. Or, for those of you with a more discriminatory taste for decorating, you can print the cards and then make a game of placing them on the correct object, and then put them away when the game is over.

➢ Practice printing letters, cut them apart, and then lay them together to make words.

➢ Develop a stack of note cards with familiar words. Stretch a string so that sentences can be formed by hanging the words together using clothes pins.

➢ Sell books that have become ho-hum to a used book store and shop for new and more challenging ones.

> If your child just wants to flip through a book and look at the pictures now and then, go along with it. This is usually a sign that you are about to hear a question that hopefully you'll hear time and time again—one that should be music to your ears because it is an indicator of readiness to learn:

What is this word?

Simple Strategies to Encourage Comprehension

To improve reading comprehension, make a habit of having your child retell the story. If that seems too difficult, flip through the book again and use the pictures as a prompt. Don't forget to take "your turn," during which you can have some fun by adding some ridiculous details to see if he or she can catch you.

To develop thinking skills, ask stimulating questions along the way. *What do you think is going to happen? What would you do if this were happening to you? If you were in this story, which character would you like to be?* Take turns making up alternate endings, and compare the book to other stories you've read or events that have happened in real life.

Most importantly, don't forget to have fun adding theatrics to your voices when the speaker changes. Your child will work hard at comprehending what is going on to put the right feeling into the words.

Word Recognition

Reading fluency increases with the number of words that are "instantly recognized." These are words that become so familiar that there is no hesitation in reading, pronouncing, or processing their sound and meaning. These words can become even more powerful when you practice using them in the following two ways:

> As words become familiar, print them individually on cards or pieces of paper. Concoct new sentences by arranging the words in different sequences.
> As soon as you hit an unfamiliar word, try asking one or more of these questions:

What letter does the word begin with?
What sound does the first two (or three) letters make?
Can we figure it out by looking at the picture?
What word would make sense?

Don't agonize over every single word. It's okay to just blurt it out rather than allowing reading together to become a chore. There are many words that have to be flat-out memorized, rather than sounded out, especially "Dolch" words.

What are "Dolch" words?

Back in the 1930's, a man named E.W. Dolch began working on compiling a list of words most frequently appearing in children's books. Most of the words cannot be illustrated in a picture or sounded out by using the usual phonetic methods. These "high-frequency words" must be memorized or recognized on "sight," hence the more familiar term, "sight words." [47]

Over the years, professionals have tinkered with the original lists, (Dolch kept changing his mind about which words to include as well), and many versions continue to surface; however, most vary by only a few words. If you are regularly reading children's books together, you are probably already doing enough to introduce and teach these words. I wouldn't worry about doing anything further unless the teacher hands you a list to practice at home.

For those of you that are curious and/or antsy about what those words might be, I've included a sample list. You can also find an abundance of websites that not only provide similar lists, but also flashcards and other learning tools you can download and print for use at home.

Sample list to master prior to entering kindergarten:

a, and, away, big, blue, can, come, down, find, for, funny, go, help, here, I, in, is, it, jump, little, look, make, me, my, not, one, play, red, run, said, see, the, three, to, two, up, we, where, yellow, you

Sample list for kindergartners to master prior to first grade:

all, am, are, at, ate, be, black, brown, but, came, did, do, eat, four, get, good, have, he, into, like, must, new, no, now, on, our, out, please, pretty, ran, ride, saw, say, she, so, soon, that, there, they, this, too, under, want, was, well, went, what, white, who, will, with, yes

(Suggested reading: *A Funny Dolch Word Book #1: Stories, Poems, Word Search Puzzles* by Betsy B. Lee. She has also written "Book #2" and "Book #3" which are all written for ages 4 through 8. Also: *The Cat in the Hat*, by Dr. Seuss, which contains nothing *but* Dolch words.)

Don't overlook everyday opportunities for reading enrichment.

> Check out the weather report in the newspaper together before picking out clothes for an outing.
> Study the written details in catalogs even if you are just "wishing" together.
> Learn to love the Sunday comics again.
> Turn on the closed caption feature on your TV every now and then. You can see that even the silly sounds that cartoon characters make can be written in words.
> Help your child write down things to remember such as items you need to buy for school.
> Again, use the newspaper, telephone book, Internet, and other sources to show how you can find information for things such as planning a vacation.

What is the deal with a child who seems obsessed with one particular book?

Even though you may get tired of reading or hearing the same story over and over again, there could be some value in doing so. Elaine McEwan-Akins, an educational consultant, believes that children love the "sense of power" in knowing what is printed on each page.[48] According to researchers at the University of Texas, there could also be something very complex happening in your child's brain. They believe that young minds cannot integrate and process all the details of an interesting tale the way we can, so thinking about it over and over again helps accomplish this. Eventually, when a child tires of the story, it is because he or she has finally produced a full-blown mental movie that has become tiresome.[49] Until then, grin and bear it, or get someone else to suffer through the umpteenth reading.

Should you allow your child to pretend to read a book that he or she has memorized?

Yes, especially if you are working your way through a challenging book and your child gets tired. It's good to have one that you can pull out when you need a confidence builder. Zipping through it may provide the stress relief needed after working on something a little harder.

A Word about Learning to Print

As soon as your child shows an interest in learning to print, you need to find out what official style your school district endorses. The guidance counselor, principal, or any teacher should be able to give you that information. The two basic types are D'Nealian and Zaner-Bloser, and all the others are variations of one or the other or a combination of the two. (Just think about all the different fonts available on a computer.) Proponents of the D'Nealian style, which has a "curly cue" look to it, believe it makes the transition to cursive writing much easier. Those in the Zaner-Bloser camp, which consists of traditional "sticks and balls" strokes, argue that it is easier to master and supports reading success because it looks similar to fonts in books.

There are a multitude of free practice sheets in both styles available online that can be downloaded and printed, or you can find them in many stores, but don't go wild. Your child should be able to print his or her first name before kindergarten, plus a few letters of the alphabet, but that's it. Anything beyond that shouldn't be forced. On the other hand, if the challenge appears to be "fun" then provide lots of doodling materials and guidance. (Suggested websites: www.handwritingworksheets.com and www.handwritingforkids.com)

Your job is primarily to:

➤ Set up a place to practice by providing a booster seat or tall chair at an adult-sized work station, or a child-sized desk or table and chair. Sitting in a comfortable and balanced position is necessary for proper hand control.
➤ Demonstrate the correct way to grip a writing utensil in the dominant hand while steadying the paper with the opposite hand.
➤ Provide examples to trace or copy.

➢ Demonstrate the correct direction of strokes and how words are written from left to right. It can be helpful to "guide" your child's hand with your own, or draw directional arrows around sample letters.

➢ Do not discourage scribbling. Its merits are two-fold: It helps develop hand control and relieves tension.

If you're a go-getter, here are some other ideas for expanding learning while learning to print:

➢ Buy a three-ring binder and a three-hole punch. Learning to manipulate the hole-punch and placing papers in the binder builds fine motor skills, plus you're less likely to go crazy with papers flying everywhere. Putting papers in a binder will also give you the opportunity to examine and point out the progress made in learning to print legible letters. Or, if you don't want to make that much of an effort and don't mind spending a little more money, buy a scrapbook with the "top loadable" clear sleeves. You can easily slide in all kinds of work you choose to save.

➢ To help encourage the connection between speaking and writing, have your child "dictate" messages that need to be written down. Print them in the appropriate style to be copied or read back for clarity. Don't forget to add details such as the time the message was written. Time is a difficult concept to grasp, but the more you talk or write about it, the clearer it becomes.

➢ You can develop time awareness by having your child look at a calendar to copy the month and day on each practice paper. Once he or she can do this without help, you'll know you're making progress.

➢ Assist in labeling artwork or pages in coloring books with simple descriptions such as "yellow cat," as well as "signing" creations, in the right, bottom corner, the same way an artist would.

➢ Be creative in looking for opportunities to practice. Kids love sidewalk chalk, writing in pudding so they can lick their fingers, and scribbling on steamy windows.

➢ Distinguish between capital and lower case letters. Stick to the basic capitalization rules, i.e., the first word in a sentence, names, and the pronoun "I".

➢ Provide a large eraser for practice. The eraser tip on the end of a pencil is too difficult to master at this age. Being able to erase without wrinkling or tearing a hole in the paper is a good sign that fine motor skills are developing.

➤ In the early stages of learning letters and learning to print, you can make it easier and more enjoyable by "printing" in the sand, using finger-paint, or by forming letters with manipulatives such as cereal, candy, or other small items.

➤ Once you get going, encourage daily journaling by providing sentences to copy. Simple entries such as, "I played with Ted," are perfect for this age group. Whatever you do, don't ever throw it away. The sentimental value will increase with time.

Sneaky Ways to Increase Math Skills

Put away those flash cards and relax. You'll kill the joy of learning and your child will start hiding from you if you think you have to continuously drill, drill, drill. Kids will pick up math skills if, again, you treat them like people and not like inanimate objects. Utilize everyday opportunities as they present themselves.

> ➤ Setting the table and preparing meals involves a multitude of opportunities to "count," and children love to feel needed. *How many baked potatoes do you think I should make? If we give each person two napkins, how many napkins will we need? How many pieces of cake should I cut so that everyone will get one piece? If Daddy wants two bread sticks and we only want one, how many should I bake?*
> ➤ When you read together, point out and say the page numbers.
> ➤ You can use shopping trips to show how different items have different values. Place a limit on spending before you go, and then point out what your child can purchase right then, and how many trips to the store, or weeks he or she would have to wait to purchase more expensive things. This will also teach the payoff of "impulse control."
> ➤ Play games that involve counting. Look for age appropriate board games to purchase. Designers have come up with ideas that are way cooler than when you were a child.
> ➤ If adults or older children are playing board or card games, the two of you can sit together and play as a team.
> ➤ Place magnetic numbers and plus and minus symbols on the refrigerator to play with.
> ➤ Cut cheese and other foods into geometric shapes such as triangles, circles, squares, and rectangles.
> ➤ Divide up food into halves, thirds, fourths, etc.

> Buddy up when you're going to use a tape measure, thermometer, the bathroom scale, etc. There are all kinds of mathematical applications to be learned.

> Look for road signs bearing numbers. *If Zanesville is 10 miles away and Cambridge is 30 miles away, which town will we get to first?*

> Take advantage of situations in which you can teach mathematical concepts. For instance, you could start out by saying, *I'm guessing that we'll be there in 30 seconds. Let's count to 30 and see if I'm right!* As you progress, you can step up the challenge. For example: *I'm guessing that we'll be there in one more minute. There are 60 seconds in a minute. Let's count to 60 and see if I'm right!*

> There are an abundance of free interactive "math" games available on line for every grade level. There are also instructional sites that will be very helpful as your child gets older. All you have to do is perform a search for the mathematical function you are performing such as "adding fractions" and you will immediately find the pages of instruction you will need.

(Suggested reading: *Roar!: A Noisy Counting Book* by Pamela Duncan Edwards, *Addition Annie* by David Gisler, and *The Icky Bug Counting Book* by Jerry Pallotta.)

How to Have a Productive Parent-Teacher Conference

When you schedule your appointment, ask how long the meeting is expected to last. Teachers will be meeting with nearly every parent, so don't be disappointed to find out that your time slot may be relatively short. If it is any consolation, more time is generally scheduled for parents who could be facing some serious problems.

To maximize your time, be prepared with the questions that you want to ask and an open mind. It is frustrating for a teacher to attempt to describe the stumbling blocks that are getting in the way of learning when a parent appears closed to the idea that the child might be the one with the problem. It is understandable that you might feel offended by suggestions that seem to question your parenting style, but try not to take offense. The whole idea behind conferences is to exchange information and share ideas in order to support one another.

Conversely, you may be pleasantly surprised to find out that your child takes on a much different personality, spirit of cooperation, and work ethic than at home. I've had a few giggles with parents who were surprised to learn that their whiny, stubborn brat is a perfectly well-adjusted, agreeable angel at school. Of course the flip side of this is a child who is tough to teach, but is perfectly agreeable at home. Whatever you do, be humble and pleasant. If the teacher reports to the principal that you were difficult, then the two most important people you need to deal with will be on the defensive when they see you coming.

No matter what the outcome of your conference, you will come away with the information you need if you focus on the following topics. Use these suggestions to help you formulate the questions you may want to ask:

Is he/she ahead or behind the average student?

This is a good way to gauge just how well things are going. "About the same" doesn't necessarily mean anything negative. "Average" means that everything is going well, in fact, it may be going so well that the teacher doesn't really have much to say.

What are his/her strengths and weaknesses?

This will let the teacher know that you are going to be receptive to the bad news as well as the good.

Do you have any suggestions for me?

Do you need to provide any supplemental help, such as extra reading time at home? Are there any social or behavioral problems you can address to support the teacher?

Does he/she get along with others?

Developing emotional intelligence should be just as important to you as academic success. Don't slough off any negative comments. Think about the difficult people you have to deal with in your life. There's still time for an attitude adjustment. (See *Making Friends* for additional help.)

Does he/she follow directions and rules?

If not, ask for specifics. You can mimic the same rules at home until it sinks in while demonstrating support for the teacher.

Has he/she ever met with the principal, nurse, or guidance counselor?

Sometimes students become members of our "frequent flyer club" without your knowledge. If these trips occur because of constant petty issues, i.e., chronic complaining about stomachaches, crying jags, or "potential" discipline problems, we may not let you know about each and every incident until it becomes a serious problem. Conferences are the perfect time to find out if we need your help in curtailing what could escalate into something that interferes with academic progress.

Is there anyone else you think I should talk to while I'm here?

Other professionals are usually available during conferences to support and/or supplement the teacher's efforts such as the special education director, speech therapist, and guidance counselor. In addition, you will have the opportunity to meet teachers of non-academic subjects such as art, music, and physical education if you wish.

Are you missing any paperwork, fees, or permission slips from me?

You want to make sure that everything is finding its way home and back.

Other Suggestions:

Don't be embarrassed to ask for clarification of educational jargon.

The purpose of the conference is for us to help you better understand how you can support our efforts, not to confuse you by using unfamiliar terms. Please don't be embarrassed to speak up when we do that. Occasionally we need to be reminded that not everyone is acquainted with the vocabulary we use on a daily basis.

I was once blindsided in a meeting when a mother began sobbing after being told that her son was outstanding in his regular classes as well as in his "specials." The term "specials" is teacher slang for classes that are considered enrichment subjects outside of core academics such as art, music, and physical education. She thought that somehow her son had been placed in special education classes for learning disabled students without her knowledge.

If you are curious or concerned about what is being taught, ask for information about the "state standards."

Teachers can no longer be loosey-goosey about what they are doing in their classrooms. As previously outlined in the section about understanding test scores, states now have strict guidelines about what should be taught in each academic area. Many schools have stopped providing hard copies of these materials to parents because of the cost and/or because they are usually available on your state's department of education website.

If you take the time to look them over, it will help you support learning at home. For example, a standard for kindergartners in science might be to "understand that changes in the weather are caused by interconnected events and cycles in our universe." Even though this may sound complicated, the benchmarks leading up to that understanding will simplify it for you. They may include: Naming the four seasons, describing weather patterns and temperatures that are typical for each season, and being able to describe weather conditions as they occur. *(It is hot and sunny today, but it might rain because I see some dark clouds.)*

Try to frame your questions in a non-accusatory fashion to avoid putting the teacher on the defensive.

Not: *What are you doing all day long that you can't teach my kid to read?*
But rather: *What can we do to help my child become a better reader?*

Unless you're trying to break into the entertainment industry, don't ever say: *My kid doesn't lie.*

While that may be somewhat true, all kids, at the very least, will exaggerate, omit details, or paint their own pictures to stay out of trouble. Don't we all? So never make such a silly statement because it will inevitably be repeated in the teacher's lounge.

Remember that listening is just as important as talking.

Don't spend too much time trying to explain what you view as the problem and how you think it can be solved. Conferences should be a two-way street. Plus, the more cooperative the parent, the harder the teacher will be apt to work for the benefit of the child. Teachers don't intend to be this way; it's human nature.

If there are any touchy issues that need to be addressed, the teacher will no doubt be prepared to discuss them. Do not dwell on petty problems, eating up the time that may be needed for a more important discussion. If you have time left, you can always back-paddle.

Ask what mode of communication the teacher prefers.

Every teacher is different, so there is nothing wrong with being up front and asking what would be the least intrusive way to communicate. Some prefer to send notes back and forth in backpacks, some prefer phone calls during their preparation time, some function best through email, and some like to set up face-to-face meetings. Parents who show respect for a teacher's boundaries are certain to create a positive working relationship.

Please be sensitive about the time you spend bending the teacher's ear.

Your child may be the center of your universe (and we certainly hope so), but it is logistically impossible for a teacher to listen to microscopic details about the lives of every student. It would also be advisable for you to pay attention to how much time you spend chattering about academic problems. Occasionally there are parents who want to talk, talk, talk, when they might be able to solve the problem just by taking the time to assist with homework or by taking the initiative to spend extra practice time at home.

Find out if the school hosts a website for parents to check on individual progress.

The process is simple. You will be assigned a username and password to access all kinds of information from any computer. If you don't own a computer or know how to use one, you can visit your local library for help.

Typical programs list assignments, grades, attendance records, and even teacher comments.

Attend functions such as Back-to-School Night, Open House, and Parent-Teacher Organization meetings.

Your attendance will prove that you are truly interested in promoting a spirit of cooperation. More importantly, you will have the opportunity to learn the details of events and activities that teachers normally do not have the time or the resources to let you know about. Getting the chance to look at student displays of work can also be interesting. It gives you the opportunity to make a visual comparison of how your child measures up to his or her peers.

These events are usually announced via school newsletters or posted on the general school website.

Volunteer your time or resources to show your support for the school.

If your schedule makes it difficult to attend functions and fundraisers, there are other things you can do to help out:

> Put together a duplicate pack of school supplies and give it to the teacher. It will feel like a windfall for a disadvantaged student or a new student who arrives in the middle of the year.
> Ask the teacher for a list of materials that are often used for class projects, such as egg cartons, and start rounding them up.
> Offer to care for classroom pets and critters over weekends and holidays.
> Find replacements for classroom animals that die.
> Provide snacks for a special event.
> Make phone calls to recruit others, such as grandparents and community members, to tutor, assist in the classroom, or work at school functions.
> Contact businesses for supplies and donations.

Gets the facts before you react.

Children paint their own pictures of a situation. Sometimes they only tell you half of the story and sometimes the half they tell you isn't true. I remember all too well the big stink that ensued after a teacher allegedly screamed and threw "Charlie" across the classroom. After a huge brouhaha, it was discovered that Charlie was a puppet sitting on the teacher's desk that apparently had a hairy spider crawling across his face.

The worst thing you can do is buddy up with another disgruntled parent before you know for sure that there is a definite problem. I have witnessed more situations than I care to count in which someone has embellished an unhappy or disappointing situation and attempted to bamboozle others to gather support. Do your own investigating before jumping on a band wagon headed for trouble.

Talk directly to the teacher before you decide what action you'll take. If you contact the superintendent first, he or she will expect the principal to handle the situation anyway. If you start with the principal, then he or she will have to talk to the teacher before taking action, so you're better off going straight to the source of your problem in the first place. Whatever you do, don't show up at a school board meeting armed with misinformation, or write an emotionally charged "letter to the editor" in the local newspaper. You'll risk personal embarrassment and diminished credibility as a community member.

When you're feeling good about the teacher, say so!

Teachers are human beings. The power of positive reinforcement can enhance their effectiveness just like anyone else. When your child makes a nice comment about something, write a note of appreciation. If you can't resist sending a little gift, you can't miss with a container of anti-bacterial wipes or a box of anti-viral tissues.

The squeaky wheel does indeed get the grease, but don't overdo it.

Contact with the teacher will benefit your child. Not overbearing, aggressive contact, but a reasonable amount of interaction accompanied by your willingness to bear some of the responsibility when changes are needed.

Straight Talk about Special Education

It is difficult to diagnose kindergartners with learning disabilities or behavior disorders because symptoms are typically characteristic of immature children in general.[50] Learning problems may be the result of a brain processing problem, but then again, it could be due to a lack of intellectual stimulation prior to entering school. Or, a child could simply be a later bloomer who needs another year to mature before moving on to first grade.

A behavior disorder could be caused by some type of yet-to-be-diagnosed physical or mental condition, but then again, bad behavior at this age could be the result of overly permissive or doting parents, or being reared in a dysfunctional, abusive, or unstructured home. When you factor in the impact of emotional trauma (divorce, death, moving, etc.), genetics, poor nutrition, and exposure to all the everyday negative influences that are out there, it's a wonder that any child turns out halfway normal. For these reasons, the act of a teacher or parent initiating psychological testing for a kindergartner is a controversial issue.

Now for the good news...

Whatever the problem may be, you should take comfort in the fact that the teacher will most definitely be in your corner when it comes to finding a solution. Special education services are now so sophisticated and regulated by law that the goal of helping students "catch up" with their peers is much more attainable than ever. In fact, the first priority is no longer initiating testing, but trying various "interventions" in case a little extra support is all that is really needed to get a student back on track.[51]

These interventions usually entail a little extra help in the classroom, and/or some things you can do at home. Some examples for this age group include:

- ➤ Sitting near the teacher's desk for extra help in staying on task.
- ➤ Arranging for additional practice printing, reading, or working math problems with a classroom volunteer, intervention specialist, and/or parent.
- ➤ Providing constant positive reinforcement for appropriate behavior while ignoring as many inappropriate behaviors as possible.
- ➤ Giving directions in steps as tasks are completed, rather than all at once.
- ➤ Providing extra help during a group activity that seems to be emotionally overwhelming and/or teeming with distractions.
- ➤ Removing all unnecessary and distracting items from the student's workspace.
- ➤ Being paired up with an organized and industrious peer who will be encouraging and helpful.

It only makes sense that a teacher would experiment with a significant number of possible remedies before engaging the school district's professionals in initiating formal testing for a disability. You may, of course, request a formal evaluation at any time, but if sound reasons can be provided for not doing so, you will be denied.[52]

The proper procedure is for the teacher to first communicate to you that a significant problem has surfaced and what remedies are currently being employed. If the problem continues, then you will be invited to meet with a "response to intervention team," also referred to as the "RTI Team," which is made up of professionals in the district trained to address learning problems. The idea behind this is to bring as much expertise as possible to the table to come up with additional strategies and evaluate the success of those already attempted. This team will also determine how soon they will need to meet again so that if adequate progress is not made, they can further study the problem.

In the past, if a learning disability was suspected, educators normally proceeded right away with testing. The U.S. Department of Education explains on their website why we now delay testing. In layman's terms, their position is this:

Scientific research shows that using alternate teaching strategies can often help children who are not truly learning disabled overcome their problems.[53]

What happens when testing is initiated?

Once there is significant information suggesting there might be an identifiable disability, school officials will initiate a complete child study, referred to as an MFE (Multi-Factored Evaluation). Once the examination is completed, You will review the results with the school psychologist and everyone else who participated in the evaluation. This "Evaluation Team Report," or "ETR," includes a summary of the entire evaluation process and recommendations. If your child qualifies for special education services, an IEP (Individual Education Plan) will be put together to employ a rigorous plan of action with intervention specialists and/or other appropriate personnel. The goal is to develop and implement strategies for overcoming or compensating for learning and/or behavior problems.

If you want to educate yourself about the procedures that will be followed and/or your legal rights, you can obtain a resource guide for parents from the Special Education Coordinator in your district. It will also outline what the Individuals with Disabilities Education Act requires of schools.[54]

What is included in an Individual Education Plan?

The design of the program depends upon specific needs, but the general format includes:

> The student's current "level of performance" in the area of concern, for example, the grade level at which he or she is currently reading.

> Specific annual goals, as well some short-term objectives to be reached along the way.

> The specific services that will be provided. For example, a student may receive speech therapy once a week, and work with an intervention specialist daily on academic skills.

> The extent to which the student will be included in a regular classroom, and the extent to which he or she will need to meet with a specialist in another room, if at all.

> The date that the IEP will go into effect, and the date at which it will be up for "review." An IEP is generally in effect for one year, but may be reviewed and modified as soon as it is determined that something needs to be changed and/or added.

How can you be sure that the teacher will challenge your child and not make things too easy?

The days are long gone when the objectives for special education students were merely focused on helping them obtain a "productive and meaningful place in society." Now the focus is on determining what kind of help students need to be able to compensate for learning problems so they can pursue the most rigorous academic regimen possible.

Federal regulations do not allow schools any wiggle room no matter how severe the problem. Students are expected to make significant progress from year to year, so teachers and administrators work constantly to make adjustments to ensure that they do.[55]

What if your child does not qualify for special education services?

A teacher's success depends upon the success of his or her students, so even if a specific disability cannot be pinpointed, the search for successful remedies will continue. If a disability does exist, but it is not severe enough to warrant special education services, your child may meet the qualifications for a 504 Plan.

What is a 504 Plan?

It is the next best thing to an IEP. Students who can function in a regular classroom, but need monitoring and/or help because of an emotional or physical disability, are eligible. Section 504 of the Rehabilitation Act of 1973 is a federal law, governed by the Office of Civil Rights, that guarantees that students who need help will get it.[56] Many of the services that can be provided are similar to those provided through special education programs. In fact, 504 Plans are often written for students that no longer qualify for special education, but still need some kind of support to transition out of the program.

What if it seems obvious that something is wrong, but school officials do not feel that testing is warranted?

They may be thinking that it is merely a lack of frontal lobe development. If there was ever a solid argument for having a child repeat kindergarten, this is it. If the frontal cortex of the brain is not developed enough to handle the work, the only thing you can do is wait. It doesn't matter what kind of effort you put into homework, tutoring, drilling, or coaching, this part of the brain has to be developed to the point at which it can process the level of thinking required at this grade level.[57]

Even though school professionals can only speculate that this might be the problem, it is a very distinct possibility if all other impediments to learning have been ruled out. In layman's terms, we describe this condition as *immaturity*.

In the final analysis, if your child has entered school before he or she was emotionally, socially, or cognitively ready, what are your options?

Whatever you do, don't keep pushing educators to promote your child from grade to grade with failing marks, or attempt to bully teachers into handing over better grades than deserved. Nor should you keep shoving extra work down your child's throat every night in attempt to "fix" the problem. Some supplemental work will often get a student back up to speed, but if it never lets up, the psychological impact can defeat the purpose. Once school becomes the enemy, we're all doomed—the student, the parents, the teacher, and everyone else involved.

Open your mind and carefully consider the options that the teacher and/ or district specialists can recommend. Policies and availability of programs differ, but these are some of the possibilities:

> ➤ If kindergarten is a half-day or every-other-day program in your district, ask if your child qualifies for any full-time kindergarten programs designed to supplement learning.
> ➤ Ask if there are volunteers, teacher's aides, or other knowledgeable adults who are willing and able to provide one-on-one help if you cannot find help on your own. Sometimes individual attention is all that is needed to catch up.
> ➤ Ask if an "Intervention Specialist" is available to provide any extra help. Sometimes it can be done right in the classroom during regular class time depending upon the number of other students with more severe problems being served.
> ➤ Consider returning to, or entering, a pre-school program within the district or community.
> ➤ Finish the year with the understanding that your child will repeat kindergarten. If failure is inevitable, this is the least emotionally damaging time for repeating a grade.
> ➤ You certainly have the right to withdraw your child from school and begin anew the following year, providing you will still meet the compulsory attendance requirement in your state. If this is something you're considering, be sure to ask for an opinion from school officials first.

Remain realistic, yet hopeful, when faced with the possibility of a life-long disability.

It is a normal reaction to feel as if your entire world is about to crumble, but please consider the following:

> ➤ There are now colleges that accommodate students with learning disabilities, and the number is rising.
> ➤ Many such students are identified as "twice exceptional," meaning that it is common for a disabled child to also be gifted in other areas. For example, a child who has problems reading may be gifted artistically.
> ➤ Experts concluded in a study in 1987 that parent's perceptions of their disabled children tend to be significantly negative compared to children's perceptions of themselves. Some noteworthy examples are that students expressed more ambitious future plans for themselves, they perceived themselves to have more friends than their parents believed, their confidence level in solving their own problems was higher, and former students were not as displeased with their current jobs as their parents reported. In other words, disabled students were much happier and well-adjusted than their parents realized.[58]
> ➤ Many ultra-successful people are "learning disabled" such as financier Charles Schwab, who is dyslexic.[59] He and his wife, Helen, fund Schwab Learning, a foundation that provides support and resources for struggling children and their parents. I agree with Mr. Schwab's stance that "Kids are not stupid—they just learn differently," and I hope you will too.[60]

Knowledge is power.

Most any definition of a disability can be found online, but new problems and remedies are continuously being identified. As soon as you are alerted to a possible problem, contact the district special education office for accurate and up-to-date information. You'll want to educate yourself not only about the help that can be offered in school, but what you can be doing at home to maximize success as well.

A Few Other Terms and Buzzwords

The following list is by no means inclusive of every definition related to special education, but includes some of the most commonly used words and acronyms.

ADD

Attention Deficit Disorder is characterized by those who have a tendency to drift away mentally into their own daydreams as well as those who are easily distracted by the least little thing. Either way, disorganization and failing to finish tasks are often the result. This problem alone does not qualify a student for special education services, but often leads to more serious problems if not controlled. Students with ADD do not automatically qualify for a 504 Plan either. In order to qualify under the Section 504 regulations, "the impairment must substantially limit a major life activity," which in this case would be "learning."[61]

ADHD

Those who have Attention Deficit/Hyperactivity Disorder are constantly distracted, not just by outside stimuli, but by their own incessant need to be constantly moving. This impulsivity component is a child's worst enemy because it causes behavioral problems. As with ADD, some parents resort to medication when all else fails. I am not a proponent of medication, but if every avenue has been explored as far as diet and modifications, you may not have any other choice. If you ever get to that point, be sure to stay in close contact with both the teacher and physician to be sure that it is making a positive difference.

(Suggested reading: *Jumpin' Johnny Get Back to Work!: A Child's Guide to ADHD/Hyperactivity* by Michael Gordon.)

At Risk

A child who is "at risk" should be monitored closely because of the high probability of developing problems that could adversely affect learning.

Cognitive

"Cognitive" problems refer to the inability to comprehend, reason, or process information. Cognitive processing or functioning basically means the ability to "think."

Congenital

Refers to a problem that is present at birth.

Delay

A delay is indicative of something a child cannot understand or cannot do that is expected of most children of the same age. Sometimes it is an isolated problem that can be fixed with extra stimulation or attention, but sometimes it is a warning that other problems with skill development may surface.

Deficit

A lower level of performance than should be expected for a child of the same age.

Developmentally Delayed

Refers to a child who acquires skills later than the expected age.

Dyslexia

Dyslexia is a learning disability that involves difficulties in processing words and numbers. It is much more complex and varied than the typical notion that "dyslexics" simply see words and/or letters "backwards." It is not curable, nor outgrown, but those who have it are usually of average or above average intelligence, so they are able to learn ways to compensate for this impairment with the help of a learning specialist.[62]

(Suggested reading: *Thank You, Mr. Falker* by Patricia Polacco.)

Identified

This is educational slang meaning that a student has qualified for special education services. He or she has been *identified* as having a disability.

Inclusion

This is the practice of providing support services to special education students while attending regular classes, rather than receiving instruction in another room.

Least Restrictive Environment

This is one of the mandatory components of developing an IEP. The child must be placed in a setting in which he or she will be best educated, meaning an environment with as few roadblocks as possible.

Mainstreaming

This is the practice of putting special education students in regular classes in which they can be successful without any extra help.

Modification

Any change that is made in instruction or in the school environment to meet a child's special education needs.

OHI

Other Health Impairment refers to chronic or acute medical conditions that have been diagnosed by a licensed physician that could adversely affect learning. Some examples are epilepsy, diabetes, asthma, allergies, and leukemia.

(Suggested reading: *Stevie's New Blood* by Kathryn Ulberg Lilleby; *Allie the Allergic Elephant: A Children's Story of Peanut Allergies* by Nicole Smith; *Zooallergy: A Fun Story about Allergy and Asthma Triggers, Taking Asthma To School,* and *Taking Diabetes to School,* by Kim Gosselin.)

OT

Occupational Therapy is often provided for students who need intensive help with manipulating their hands and fingers. (Occupational therapists are also referred to as "OTs.")

Pull-out

A term used to describe the act of taking the student out of the regular classroom for extra academic help or some kind of therapy in another setting with a specialist.

PT

Physical Therapy is often provided for students with physical problems that can be related to learning problems. (Physical therapists are also referred to as "PTs.")

Related Services

"Related Services" are documented in an IEP and refer to things that are provided other than academic instruction such as speech therapy, physical therapy, or even special transportation arrangements.

Remedial Reading or Math

This is instruction that is arranged for a student who has fallen behind, but it is not necessarily a part of a special education program.

Self-contained Classroom

This is a classroom that only serves students with disabilities.

Title One Program

This is not a special education program, but is often mentioned in special education meetings because it is a successful tool that prevents students who just need an extra boost from being "identified." It is the largest federally funded program in schools, aimed at helping students who need assistance beyond regular classroom instruction in reading, language arts, and math. Schools differ in the grade levels and subjects served depending upon academic needs and the amount of funding that is available. As strange as it sounds, the amount of money a district is allocated is determined by the number of students who qualify for free or reduced price lunches.[63]

TBI

Traumatic Brain Injury is the identifier for students who have suffered either an injury or illness that has adversely affected brain functioning.

Nurturing an Independent Thinker/ Problem Solver

Sometimes we get so caught up in teaching, coaching, and directing that we inadvertently fail to nurture creative and constructive thinking. We want our children to believe what we believe, we want them to do what we want, we want to spare them the pain of getting hurt, and we want to prevent them from making mistakes. At the same time, we want them to have the confidence to try and make good decisions on their own and express their ideas.

Show respect for different tastes, opinions, and ideas.

If we all liked the same things, the world would be a pretty boring place. The lines would be insufferably long too, so the next time you're out together, point this out. *I'm glad not everyone wanted to see this movie, or it would have been sold out. Let's eat at Mommy's favorite restaurant tonight and then next weekend we'll let you pick a place. Whoever thought up this game must be really creative because it is so much fun to play.*

Don't try to pound a square peg through a round hole.

Don't try to live vicariously through your child because you didn't get to do what you wanted or because you didn't excel the way you could have when you were young. If your little girl would rather play soccer than take ballet lessons, let her. If your son would rather play a violin than play football, so be it. Save your arguing for things that really matter.

Ask thought provoking questions.

Do you think we'll be able to see any stars tonight? How could we cool down the house without turning on the air conditioning? How long do you think it would take us to "pick" the grass instead of mowing it? Do you think we could walk to Africa? Do you think this watermelon would float in your pool? What if we could only walk backwards, or what if we had to hop everywhere? Which would you prefer?

Initiate a good old-fashioned debate.

Do you think boys are stronger than girls? What is the worst tasting food in the world? Should kids have to wear bicycle helmets? Should everyone be able to decide on his or her own bedtime? Should you always tell the truth, even when it hurts someone's feelings?

When you have the necessary patience and time, stop pulling rank and answer a question with a question instead of saying, "Because I said so."

Why do you have to go to bed? What would happen if I let you stay up as long as you wanted? You don't want to take a bath? What would happen if you stopped taking baths? What would you smell like? What would your skin feel like?

Make predictions, even if it is just for fun.

Peter Rabbit's mother just told him not to go into Mr. McGregor's garden. What do you think will happen if he goes in there anyway? How long do you think it will take us to make homemade butter in this small jar? Could we get it done in time for dinner? (See the section on Homemade Fun for Overachieving Parents for the recipe.)

Analyze situations.

Why do you think Peter is going into the garden even though his mother just told him not to? Tap your spoon on the side of these water glasses. Why do you think they make different sounds? (Then line them up and see if you can play a little tune.) We need to buy a birthday present for Daddy and we need to stop and get some ice cream. Which should we do first?

Brainstorm to practice solving problems.

Poor Peter can't find his way out of the garden. How would you find your way back to the gate? I'm out of chocolate chips to make cookies. What else could I put in the dough that might taste good? (Then try it.) How could we clean those bugs out of the pool? (Then try it.)

Be prepared for those boring moments when you could be playing mind-challenging games.

Shop for things you can stow away in your purse or vehicle such as the *Brain Quest* cards by Chris Welles Feder. There are packs for all levels, including waterproof ones you can play with in the bathtub.

Vocalize what you're thinking as you work through your own dilemmas.

The veterinarian wants to know how much Fluffy weighs, but she is too wiggly to sit on the scale. Let's see. I could weigh myself first, and then weigh myself again while I'm holding her. Then I could subtract how much I weigh from the total to see how much Fluffy weighs! Do you think that will work?

This will also demonstrate that you don't automatically know everything and how you also have to go through the process of figuring out what to do in a quandary.

Even though it is necessary to run your home somewhat like a dictatorship, allow some flexibility.

Children should be permitted to make some personal choices. Being told what to do and how to do it every minute of the day stifles their creativity and problem-solving skills.

> ➤ Instead of getting angry in situations such as dawdling in the bathtub, throw in some toys and grab something to entertain yourself while you're waiting around.
> ➤ Choosing one's own clothing is also a harmless pleasure. If you are paranoid that staff members will think you're neglectful at the sight of a hideously mismatched getup, you couldn't be more wrong. We have to negotiate on a daily basis with tons more kids than you do, so we know the game well. If it drives you completely crazy, then match up clothes and offer choices among pre-assembled outfits.
> ➤ If you have an "independent learner" who can complete homework with minimal assistance, it shouldn't matter where it is done. I've had members of the National Honor Society tell me that they do all their studying in front of the TV. If it gets done and done well, then why shouldn't they? (Some students actually need a little background noise to concentrate.)

➤ Create a space where he or she can go wild with craft materials, age-appropriate toys with hundreds of pieces, or anything that has the propensity to drive you mad when underfoot. Spread out a sheet or thin blanket and then for a quick clean up, just grab the corners and tie a big knot and wha-la! It can be stored in a hidden place for the next time.

Home Remedies for Alleviating School Stress

What can you do to help after an upsetting day at school? A stressed-out child can often times be "fixed" in much the same way that adults shake off the occasional bad day at work. If we come home to loving arms, a favorite meal, a bubble bath, pajamas warmed up in the dryer, and most importantly, a sympathetic ear, we have a pretty good chance of recovering. But what should you do when the problem is pervasive enough to last longer than a few days?

Make sure that there is truly a problem.

If crying, temper tantrums, or sulking is the only method of getting your attention, then why wouldn't your child use these things to manipulate you? Maintain a running dialog every day to prevent this from happening. Be just as interested in the good stuff as the bad. *How was your day? Who did you play with at recess? Was anyone extra nice to you today? How did you get along with Mrs. Mellinger today? Did you enjoy your lunch? Did you read any good stories? Were you happy with the work you did? Were you proud of yourself today?*

Just like you, every little frustrating thing can wear down a child emotionally. Not being able to open a packet of ketchup, a skinned knee, a broken pencil—it can all contribute to ruining a perfectly good day. The significant difference is that from a child's perspective, these things can appear catastrophic. There is also the possibility that nothing really happened. Occasional bad moods are a fact of life. He or she may be tired, constipated, bored, or just experiencing one of those unexplainable streaks of discontent. Don't make too big of a deal out of a little spell of unhappiness unless one or more of the following behaviors persist:

➤ Getting up in the middle of the night and/or having nightmares.
➤ Loss of appetite or stress eating.
➤ Complaining of a stomachache without throwing up.
➤ Frequently crying real tears.
➤ Being abnormally aggressive with siblings and pets.
➤ "Acting out" or displaying bratty behavior.
➤ Gritting teeth while mishandling or throwing objects.
➤ Doesn't seem interested in toys or socializing.

Learning to deal with life's disappointments is a normal and necessary part of growing up.

Take advantage of opportunities to teach ways to process setbacks in a healthy way. Acknowledge disappointments without brushing them off as "no big deal." Conversely, you don't want to blow them out of proportion either. If you try to micro-manage every negative experience, you'll be taking away opportunities for emotional growth. You'll just prolong the agony of learning to deal with a world that can be pretty cruel at times. Sometimes the best fix is a huge bear hug, a few tissues, and acknowledging, *That is so sad.* This can also be an opportunity to teach healthy ways to express anger.

➤ Say that it's OK to feel upset. It is a perfectly normal feeling. We can't feel happy unless we know what it is like to feel unhappy

➤ Do not discourage crying when it is obviously a genuine response and not forced for attention. We release excess adrenaline through our tears which has a calming effect.[64]

➤ Don't discount the feeling by saying things such as, *Wait until you grow up…then you'll really have problems.* Something may seem insignificant to you, but that is because you have learned to process and work at solving or ignoring your problems. Say instead: *What happened is really bothering you, isn't it? Sometimes we have trouble forgetting about bad things that happen, and sometimes those things creep back into our heads even though we don't want them to. Whenever you feel like talking about it, just tell me. And if you have any questions, I will try to answer them the best I can.*

➤ Use exercise to "burn off" bad feelings. If you play hard enough and long enough, your body will release endorphins, which produces feelings of euphoria. [65]

➤ Tell the truth. Say that the grown-ups running the school are probably doing the best they can to help solve problems, but there are some things they can't fix. We just need to figure out how to best deal with it.

> ➢ Do not call other children names. Stick with how the perpetrator's behavior makes your child feel.

Say: *It sounds like you feel left out and sad when Anna won't play with you. Why don't you see if you can find someone else to play with? Maybe there is someone who feels left out like you do and you can help make him or her feel better.*

Don't say: *That Anna is a spoiled brat, isn't she? You ought to tell her that you don't want to play with her anyway!*

Demonstrate that failure can be a good thing.

Use your own mistakes as an example. Point out that you tried, you goofed, you learned something, and you're going to try again. Talk about how failure is actually success if you are making progress or figuring out a way to backtrack and fix what you've messed up. Best of all, if we can learn to laugh at our mistakes, failure can even be funny.

(Suggested reading: The Junie B. Jones series of books by Barbara Park are a fabulous collection of stories dealing specifically with the lighter side of stress for this age group.)

Don't forget that failure helps us discover who we really are.

Always being last in a race may mean that we can't run that fast, but it doesn't mean we're not good at other things.

When you think about it, stress at school isn't all that much different from the stress we put up with at work.

With that in mind, how do you deal with the following issues?

- ➢ Not everyone is going to like you or want to play with you.
- ➢ You are not going to be invited to all the parties you hear about.
- ➢ There will always be someone who is better, faster, or smarter than you.
- ➢ Sometimes people get praise and rewards for things that you are doing too, but nobody noticed.
- ➢ Some people will be liked just because they are cuter than you.
- ➢ There are people who will get you in trouble and won't admit it.
- ➢ Some scoundrels will take credit for your work or cool ideas.
- ➢ Some people will be mean to you when you don't deserve it.
- ➢ Some people will say hurtful things about you that aren't true.

> Sometimes people will take your stuff without asking and get away with it.
> Some people never take turns or share anything.
> There are times when you work your heart out and you still can't do it right, but you know you have to keep trying.

Your child may benefit by talking to someone who understands the injustices of everyday life, and that someone may as well be you. It will be the cheapest form of therapy you'll find.

Be aware that there are usually several reasons behind an ugly outburst.

Outbursts are generally the end result of having experienced a series of negative emotions. Think about it. What if you went to work and your new shoes started hurting and you couldn't take them off? Soon after, your favorite pencil rolled off of your desk and you couldn't find it. Then you went to lunch and discovered that someone had stolen your sandwich. You spent the afternoon hungry, and you could have dealt with that, but you kept yawning because you had trouble sleeping the night before and you had a ton of work you had to get done. When it was finally time to go home, it was raining and you'd forgotten your umbrella so you ended up getting soaked. Who wouldn't be emotionally worn down after a day like that?

(Suggested reading: *Alexander and the Terrible, Horrible, No Good, Very Bad Day* by Judith Viorst.)

Listen attentively to the same stories again and again even when there doesn't seem to be a solution.

If you think you can't do anything to help, you're mistaken. Having someone acknowledge your distress is therapeutic in itself. Even we, as adults, can sometimes purge our problems if we can tell someone about our pain without feeling as if we are being judged. Another advantage of offering your child the unlimited opportunity to vent is that struggling to find the words to explain problems will increase the ability to verbalize thoughts and feelings.

Eventually you'll figure out ways to work through the problem, maybe it will dissipate on its own, or something else will take its place and you'll get to start all over again. Just be patient. Every time you work out a problem together, the two of you will be building up your child's cache of coping skills.

Don't take the joy out of uplifting moments.

Think about some of the stress you've endured during your life that ended up being worth the hassle. Make sure that you do not poison deserved pleasure. It is such a downer to hear negative comments when you deserve to feel good. No matter how tempted you are, resist the urge to point out:

> *See? You could have been doing great all along.* Kids would like to think they are being recognized for what they've done right without someone dredging up their past failures.
> *You should be able to do this every time!* It would be nice to be able to celebrate for at least a day without having all that additional pressure heaped on your head.
> *I was proud of you, but I wish you would have worn different socks.* A comment of this nature sends the message that you will never be satisfied with any level or performance.

Make your home a welcoming sanctuary.

It is easier to survive the worst of days if you know your home will always be an emotional shelter where you'll feel loved, comforted, and cared for. Sometimes the best anesthetic is nothing more than a good laugh or time on your lap.

(Suggested reading: *Guess How Much I Love You* by Sam McBratney.)

A good night's sleep will help it all go away.

To help your little one "shake it off" enough to get the sleep that he or she so desperately needs, invoke happy thoughts.

> *What good things happened today?*
> *Who was nice to you?*
> *Did anything funny happen?*
> *Did you like your lunch?*
> *Does your bed feel cozy?*
> *Let's read a few of your favorite books before you go to sleep.*

If you can't break the cycle of negative thinking, try telling stories about bad things that happened to you as a child and how you handled it, or read books with related themes that have happy endings. The Berenstain Bears series are inexpensive and cover a wide range of topics such as bullying, problems with friends, and even the hassle of getting makeup work done.

Sometimes you just have to help your child "get through it."

Not every problem can be solved; sometimes you have no other choice than to let time and circumstances run their course. Instead of channeling all your energy into warding off the cruelties of life, spend time teaching and modeling healthy coping mechanisms.

You can go for a speedy walk together and huff and puff all your stress away. You can review what it is about certain people that irritate you and commiserate. (*That's awful! How can you stand that?*) You can give each other back rubs and tell one another how great you really are and how you don't deserve all this aggravation.

(Suggested reading: *When I Feel Sad* by Cornelia Maude Spelman.)

Keeping your family unit strong will create a mental "safety net."

In addition to maintaining familiar, everyday routines, you can strengthen your sense of family in other ways. Some examples are eating meals together, having designated seats at the table, going to church together, and celebrating birthdays with extended family members.

The Best Way to Handle a Bully

Every child has the right to feel safe at school. If you have no doubt that your child is being bullied, then you should immediately report any mental or physical abuse to the teacher, school counselor, and the principal. The bully is probably going after other kids as well, so the information you provide could give authorities the needed push to take action.

Avoid a knee-jerk reaction.

Do not march into the school with the intention of talking to the bully yourself. You will not be permitted to do so. I can't emphasize enough that you need to notify the teacher, school counselor, and the principal. Do not expect an immediate decision to be made. The person who takes the lead in this situation will need time to investigate and decide what needs to be done. Do not be upset if you aren't privy to information about how the bully is disciplined. Your main focus should be on helping keep the school safe for all children, not your opinion on what punishment would be appropriate.

To prevent retaliation, the ideal situation would be catching the bully in the act so no one will be tagged a tattle-tale. Most incidents happen in areas where students are not as closely monitored such as hallways, the cafeteria, bathrooms, or on the playground. If the attacks are happening where surveillance cameras are being used, you may be in luck because chances are, the assault has been caught on tape. If this is the case, timing is critical. Make your report immediately so the offense can easily be found without having to review oodles of footage.

Should you contact the bully's parents?

If you decide to talk to the attacker's parents outside of school, be careful about what you say. Most, but not all bullies, are victims of dysfunctional parenting, so the reaction you get may upset you even more. There are a multitude of theories as to why children become bullies, but from what I have experienced, most evolve from being around negative role models (especially older children), have hyper-critical parents who frequently use anger and aggression to get what they want, or live in a household in which physical aggression and/or verbal abuse is acceptable among family members.

There are other risks as well. If the parents haven't witnessed bad behavior at home, they may not believe you. Ironically, bullies may seem timid at home because of physically or emotionally aggressive parenting styles. There is also the possibility that the child has other issues such as feeling inadequate in some way, and then lashes out at others in order to feel superior. And lastly, you may make the situation worse by "tattling." Many children stop confiding in their parents when they become even more afraid that the bully will catch them alone. If the situation escalates, your child will lose trust in your ability to make things better and may become withdrawn. This type of secret has the power to become incredibly emotionally debilitating.

If the attacks are physical, happening off of school property, and contacting the parents has proven to be futile, then contact your local law enforcement agency. The parents of the offender will then know that you mean business.

Take notes as the situation evolves.

Write down everything you are told along with the date and time. I have learned from experience that if I write down what kids tell me, it gives them a boost of self-confidence knowing that they are being taken seriously. They experience a sense of relief knowing that someone else feels bad about the situation too. Having a written record of events also gives more credibility to the accusations so that school employees can take action much sooner.

What can you do to bully-proof your child?

Bullies love their game. Even at a young age, they can come up with all sorts of ways to torture others so if one thing doesn't get your goat, they'll try another. If they can't break you, they'll find another target, so the key is to learn to deflect their attacks so they'll move on. Coach your child to try the following tactics until you find something that works to diffuse the brand of bully you're dealing with.

> ➢ Try to be nice. Sometimes bullies are stumped by kindness and don't know what to say or do next. They may feel silly being mean to someone whom they can't get a rise out of and back off.
>
> ➢ Try to think of responses and comebacks that are likely to take all the fun out of an attack. For example, when a bully says, *I beat you! Haw,*

haw, haw, you slow poke! a good response would be, *You sure did! You can run a whole lot faster than me!*

➤ Inject some humor into the situation. *He said your ears are big? Did you tell him that everyone in your family has big ears and we can pick up radio stations from all over the world?*

➤ Ignore the bully. Practice role playing and be sure to trade places for added effectiveness. The most important thing to remember is to not make eye contact or say anything.

➤ If the situation has become so traumatizing that role playing isn't productive, then try using "sock" puppets to demonstrate what to say and do. Pull a pair of old white socks over your hands, draw a mean face on one and a nice face on the other and simulate a confrontation. If nothing else, you'll get a smile.

➤ Drill that it's OK to stand up for yourself but it is not OK to retaliate by doing something mean in return. In order to catch a bully and hope for any justice at all, you have to be totally innocent in the situation.

➤ Go over your safety plan to get away from mean people. *If you are really scared, you need to run away and look for an adult to help you. If you can't get away, scream "fire!" It will get someone's attention.*

➤ Try to find an older and responsible student who can keep an eye out for trouble when traveling to and from school. Just about everyone has had the experience of being afraid of a bully, so try to find someone who is bound to be passionate about being the hero that helps out.

➤ Be encouraging. Say how much bravery it takes to deal with this. Every little victory, even if it is just standing there until the bully walks away, will feel like a gigantic triumph.

➤ Emphasize that telling is okay. When you tell on a bully because someone might get hurt, that is different than telling on someone just to get that person in trouble.

➤ Point out that when a bully decides what game you'll play and who gets to do what, that you don't have to play. *Just walk to another part of the playground and play with someone else.*

➤ Encourage using a buddy system for insulation. Children who move around in groups are less likely to become targets. Arrange a few playdates if you must, to strengthen ties with other children.

➤ Don't say "toughen up" and leave it at that. You need to keep constant, focused, supportive and encouraging dialog going to build inner strength.

➤ Bullies are miserable people. Include them in your bedtime prayers. Pray that God will lead your particular bully to find goodness and happiness.

(Suggested reading: *Bootsie Barker Bites* by Barbara Bottner.)

Fantasizing can be a productive tool, so don't discourage it.

Don't be alarmed if you witness aggressive play depicting revengeful acts. First of all, it can be a tremendous outlet for frustration, and secondly, it may prevent something bad from happening. Part of the fantasy is mentally processing the entire event and realizing what might actually happen in the end.

Choose a favorite superhero to re-open some productive dialog, e.g., *What would you do if you were Spiderman?* You may find out that your plastic-sword-swinging maniac has a heart of gold and wants to "save everyone" from the bully.

What if your child is a bully?

There's an important difference between being assertive and being a bully. Teach and support assertive behavior so your child will avoid a lifetime of being trampled, but discourage mean-spirited behavior and retaliation. The first year of school is about the time children learn to form opinions and begin obtaining a larger vocabulary to voice them. Unfortunately, they do not know how to self-edit very well. Here are some ways to reprogram behavior:

➤ Don't back down in your parenting. If you can be overpowered or worn down, it reinforces the idea that we can get our way by being mean. If you don't correct your child, eventually the world will, and it won't be with love. It may come in one form or another—getting fired, divorced, arrested, etc.—but it will come.

➤ Avoid using physical punishment. It will send the negative message that exerting physical force is a method of dominating others.

➤ Choose teenage babysitters or other people whom your child looks up to and enlist their help in your mission.

➤ If being a bully is a power trip, then redirect the aggression into positive channels. Start by asking, *If you saw or heard someone being bullied, what would you do?* Be solid in discouraging physical force, but encourage using bravery to do things like moving between a bully and a victim.

> ➢ Solicit the help of the teacher, principal, and school counselor. They know who the bullies are and will work even harder to change bad behavior if they know you'll support their efforts and not work against them.
> ➢ Remember when I said that children will learn more from watching you than from listening to your words? Check your own behavior. How do you react and how do you sound when you don't get your way? How do you talk to and about others? Do you make prejudiced comments? Do you take mean-spirited jabs at others about weight, clothing, and the like? All of these things can be passed down as "learned behavior."
> ➢ Even though children are more likely to copy your behavior than listen to you, they do listen at times, especially when you're talking to someone else. You can send some pretty powerful messages if you "chat" with your spouse about some horrible behavior you've witnessed and what happened in the end. (Use your imagination if you must.)

If you begin to grow weary and feel like giving up, fuel your resolve by thinking about other parents who may be telling their children to stay away from your child.

What if your child isn't the bully, but hangs out with one?

It used to be difficult for me to understand why anyone would want to continue a friendship with a bully until someone asked me this:

Why do adults have so much trouble ending toxic friendships that drag them down?

In my opinion, the reasons are similar no matter how old you are.

> ➢ Rather than risk an ugly confrontation, we continue in the relationship. Putting it simply, we are "chicken" to make the break because there might be some scary repercussions.
> ➢ The bully is a part of our clique, so we put up with the grief rather than give up all our friends.
> ➢ Sometimes we just can't stop ourselves from seeking approval from someone who rarely gives it. *If this person thinks I'm cool, then I must be.*

Check into local martial arts programs.

Contrary to popular belief, these classes do not encourage aggression. The focus is on self-esteem, self-control, and respect for other people. The aim is to tame bullies by teaching them how to re-channel their anger and it builds confidence in victims. It also helps children with negative body images gain self-assurance as they achieve more and more physical agility. Best of all, when children learn not to be afraid, they gain a valuable mental edge.[66]

Confide in the school counselor.

Keep in contact with the school counselor. In addition to monitoring the situation, he or she can provide early intervention to prevent a lifetime of misery for victims and bullies alike. With the right coaching, victims can learn to deflect bullying tactics and bullies can develop better interpersonal relationships.

(Suggested reading: *Just Kidding* by Trudy Ludwig, *Words are Not for Hurting* by Elizabeth Verdick, *The Recess Queen* by Alexis O'Neill, *King of the Playground* by Phyllis Reynolds, and *Nobody Knew What to Do: A Story about Bullying* by Becky Ray McCain.)

Helping Your Child Make Friends

It is heart-wrenching to hear, *Nobody likes me…No one will play with me…* or *I don't have any friends,* but keep in mind that children are apt to judge their happiness on a day by day basis. What can seem catastrophic today could be forgotten tomorrow.

All children are bound to feel rejected from time to time, just like us. Sometimes a big hug and a little encouragement is all that is needed. (*How could anyone not like you?*) But when the feeling seems to be persistent, there are ways you can intervene and encourage the use of good people skills. In the long run, acquiring "emotional intelligence" can mean the difference between a lifetime of feeling lonely and disconnected versus having lots of friends, being well liked by co-workers, and being part of an emotionally healthy family.

One plus you may not have considered is the opportunity you will have to also make new friends with the people associated with your child. As you get to know other parents and school employees, you too may have the opportunity to develop some life-long relationships. Even though it may hurt, don't balk when one of your "new friends" suggests that your child may not be an ideal playmate. Thank anyone and everyone for information that may enlighten you. It is difficult to criticize someone else's child, especially knowing that yours could just as easily be crossed off someone's invitation list someday. Utilize others' insight to help you raise an emotionally intelligent person that people will love to be around.

Examples of poor social interaction and what you can do to help:

Becomes completely absorbed in a toy, computer game, or book while completely ignoring others.

It is important to learn to enjoy playing alone, but encouraging social interaction is just as important so you won't raise a child who completely isolates him- or herself. If the item in question is something that you own, show how it can be shared. If it can't easily be shared, remove it from the room and say, *Let's wait and play with this after Bethany goes home so the two of you can have fun while she's here.* If you are hosting a group that doesn't seem to gel very well, then suggest that they play an organized board game such as Candyland. The rules are spelled out and everyone must take turns.

Unwilling to share toys.

I'm not a proponent for making kids share everything. We all have something we covet and want everyone else to steer clear of. What you need to do is interject some "cause and effect" lessons. On the positive side of sharing, we make others feel good, and in turn, others will share with us. On the negative side, some people might ruin or lose our things, or love them so much that you have a hard time getting them back.

Some schools maintain the policy that all toys are to be left at home to prevent such problems. If "sharing" is allowed, make sure you put your child's name on all items and make sure he or she understands the risks.

At home, you should decide what will be hidden from visitors and what can be shared willingly.

(Suggested reading: *Sharing is Fun* by Joanna Cole; *Oh Brother! Someone Won't Share* by Betty Birney and Nancy W. Stevenson; *Let's Share, A Mind Your Manners Storybook* by Jillian Harker, which includes reward stickers; and *The Quiltmaker's Gift*, by Jeff Brumbeau.)

Tattles

This one is tricky in that children don't want to be pegged a squealer, but they enjoy pointing out bad behavior because it can make them feel superior. Practice good responses to navigate around problems. *If you push me down again, I'm not going to play with you.*

(Suggested reading: *Tattlin' Madeline* by Carol Cummings, *A Bad Case of Tattle Tongue* by Julia Cook, or *Don't Squeal Unless It's a Big Deal: A Tale of Tattletales* by Jeanie Franz Ransom.)

Hits or throws temper tantrums instead of using words to express negative feelings.

You'll be forever punishing your child for this if you don't interject a little lesson about more appropriate behavior. Start with a dialog about what should have been said instead of throwing a hissy fit. For example:

> *I feel angry that you're not sharing your crayons. I don't have anything to color with.*
> *I'm getting mad because you're not following the rules. I don't want to play this game anymore if we can't play by the rules.*
> *I feel angry when you call me names. If you don't stop it, I'm not going to play with you.*
> *Stop it. I don't like what you're doing.*

Practice what to do with your body when you feel like attacking someone:

> Keep your hands to yourself. Fold your arms tight against your chest if you feel like hitting someone or throwing something.
> When you feel like kicking, jump up and down without touching anyone until the feeling goes away.
> Count to 10 slowly and take a deep breath between each number.
> Take a giant breath and blow it out slowly. You can blow the anger right out of your body!
> If you can't control yourself, walk away to where you can't hurt anyone and take your own "time out" until you calm down.
> When you get really mad, find an adult and say what happened. Let the other person talk too. If the other person won't let you talk, say, *You talk first, and then it will be my turn.*

(Suggested reading: *Where the Wild Things Are* by Maurice Sendak, or *Amazing Mallika* by Jami Parkison.)

Is a poor sport.

What do you do about a child who pouts, cries, or has an angry outburst after losing a game? The first thing you should do is examine your own attitude about good sportsmanship. You should be modeling how a person can lose and still enjoy the game. To be able to do so is a giant leap towards learning to be a winner, even when you don't win.

Follow these rules when you play together to help remedy the problem:

> No one quits in the middle of the game. (This includes not allowing Daddy to turn off the TV when his favorite team is getting squashed like a bug.)
> You cannot change the rules in the middle of the game or between games unless it benefits everyone.
> No cheating. If you don't win fair and square, you don't really win.

➢ Don't make excuses for why you lost such as, *I could have won if I'd had on my new running shoes.*

➢ Don't make loser statements such as, *I didn't really try to beat you anyway.*

➢ If you always win, you should attempt to even the playing field so you won't lose your playmate. For example, if you're faster, give your competitor a head start.

➢ Always say congratulations to the winner.

(Suggested reading: *Playing Fair, Having Fun: A Kid's Guide to Sports and Games* by Daniel Grippo.)

Is unaware of the effect of being physically overpowering.

Who wants to play with someone who always knocks you around and dominates every type of physical activity? Along the same lines are little narcissists who grab away whatever they want, leaving others speechless and empty handed. Look for dominating behaviors which are easy to correct. Just imitate your little perpetrator so he or she can see how it feels.

Is disrespectful of others' boundaries.

You probably know of at least one adult who could also use some help in this area. Watch for quirks such as:

➢ Stepping on toes.

➢ Talking too loudly, too closely, or butting into others' conversations.

➢ Crowds into others' personal space. An example would be crowding in to sit where there isn't enough room.

➢ Doesn't read body language or "social cues" that signal things such as unwanted touching.

➢ Wants to "take over" or change the rules when joining a group.

(Suggested reading: *Personal Space Camp* by Julia Cook.)

Doesn't know how to participate in games typical of this age, especially at recess.

A good after-school conversation starter is, *What did you do during recess today?* You should be able to find out if you need to teach your child the basic rules of a game, how to jump rope, how to play fair, take turns, etc. You may also need to "practice" what to say when you want to be included in a game.

Would it be OK if I play too? This will not be an easy thing to do, but to alleviate some of the anxiety, make sure you practice what to do if the answer is "no." Walking away with pride will save face, and will sometimes stir up some guilt within the group. Encourage your child to also ask an adult for help finding someone to play with.

Is out of shape and whines about not being able to "keep up" with peers.

It doesn't matter how cool you are, when you're out on the playground or in the backyard, you may feel rejected when you can't keep up with the pace of an activity. Kids at this age are still self-centered enough to leave you out of the loop without much remorse. It's not fair and it's not nice, but that's the way it is.

Losing weight and/or getting in shape gets harder and harder with age, so the sooner you attack the problem, the less likely it will become a lifelong sentence. Being physically fit transcends into every aspect of your life. You have more energy, more coordination, and you feel more confident about your looks. You're less likely to develop weight-related illnesses on down the road such as heart disease and diabetes. You breathe and sleep better. You have more stamina in everything you do, including desk work. You may even be able to catch the cute little girl with the pigtails on the playground, depending on how physically fit she is.

➢ Never use food as a reward or withhold it as a punishment.
➢ Keep junk food out of your house.
➢ Pack healthy lunches.
➢ If your schedule makes it impossible to avoid some fast-food meals, choose restaurants that have menus that include healthy choices. If nothing else, stick to "child portions" such as "Happy Meals" rather than ordering adult-sized meals so you can cut back on calories.
➢ Educate yourself about food. Healthy snacks can keep your metabolism revved up as long as you aren't pigging out during regular meals.
➢ Never say "diet." Just supply healthy food and lots of exercise that is disguised as pure unadulterated fun. Daily physical activity will drive up lagging energy levels.

In the meantime, intervene by practicing ways to engage others in the type of play he or she can handle.

You: *Would you like to play marbles?*
Child: *I don't know how.*
You: *I'll show you. Maybe you'll like it.*

Nurture the ability to react appropriately if the answer is no.

You: *Would you like to jump rope with me?*
Child: *No!*
You: *OK. If you change your mind or want to play something else, let me know.*

(Suggested reading: *Stanley the Bear* by Alyssa Chase Rebein.)

Is painfully shy.

If you have the chance to postpone enrollment for another year, by all means do it. If you have trouble separating at screening, separating for school will be a nightmare, so you will need to either wait out another year or take action. Sometimes a year of physical and emotional maturation will make all the difference in the world. In the meantime, keep working to provide healthy and productive contact outside your family circle.

The best way to develop self-confidence is to do the thing you fear, but there is no need to shove anyone off of a dock. Sometimes the best attack is to conquer a fear one step at a time. For example, if the only way you can get your little one to stay in a Sunday school class is to sit nearby, then do it. Just start disappearing inch by inch, week by week. Sit closer and closer to the door, go to the bathroom, step out to take a phone call, wait outside the door, then eventually start attending your own class and meet up afterwards.

Arrange playdates and outings, especially with classmates, or potential classmates if possible. The wider the circle of friends, the more comfortable he or she will feel at school.

Use magnetic, personable teenage babysitters of the same sex whenever possible. The effect of this kind of social interaction and mentoring can be incredibly uplifting for a backward child.

Once you're established with a babysitter, offer sitter services for a friend with a child near the same age. If that goes well, then you can try having the babysitter do the same thing, only this time, have the three of them go to your friend's house. If you can accomplish this, you've arranged for social interaction away from home!

Attend community activities where you can step out of sight. Most libraries offer children's programs, you can enroll in enrichment activities such as dance or tumbling lessons, join an organized sport, and attend youth group activities at church. Socially interactive events outside the home can build confidence and self-esteem. The additional windfall is that children who have something in common will be more likely to play together at school.

Avoid using the label "shy." Instead, describe the behavior in a positive light. For example, say: *Brett is cautious about new situations. He likes to check things out before joining in.*

(Suggesting reading: *I Don't Know Why—I Guess I'm Shy* by Barbara Cain.)

Is a snob.

Sometimes kids will brag or use put-downs intending to send the message, *I'm better than you, so you should feel privileged that I want to be your friend.* Kids at this age aren't smart enough to figure out that this only repels others, even though most do it because they are insecure about their own self-worth. It is important that you give ample praise for good grades, achievements, *and* positive personality traits.

Think about it. Successful leaders aren't just intelligent, they are also kind to everyone, including those in subservient positions. Insist that everyone be respected for who they are, and practice what you preach.

You can model a humble attitude by taking special care to often admire character traits in others rather than their material possessions or looks. Reinforce that you should also respect others' opinions and tastes. And lastly, be careful not to stereotype people. Home is usually the place where prejudiced feelings are acquired.

(Suggested reading: *The Berenstain Bears and the In-Crowd* by Stan Berenstain and Jan Berenstain.)

Believes that he or she is "special" to a fault.

Guard against developing unhealthy self-esteem. If you make your child feel *too* special, you're eventually going to want to knock him or her off of that towering pedestal. Those who come to expect that they should be treated like royalty eventually exhibit repulsive behaviors.

> ➤ Never having to work for anything, or getting what they want by whining, they acquire a sense of entitlement. *If I want it, I should get it.*
> ➤ Over-indulgence feeds self-centeredness, delays maturation, and promotes an inflated sense of self-importance. *I can have whatever I want, just because I want it.*

➤ Parents sometimes make the mistake of micro-managing school projects, contest entries, and even homework to the point that it becomes expected. *I deserve rewards even though I don't earn them.*

➤ When parents do not respect rules, or even "lie" for a child's advantage, it can plant a seed that says: *I am so special that I do not have to follow the rules. I can fib to get whatever I want.*

➤ Children who are told over and over again that they are superior in looks may equate outward appearance with self-worth. It can become ultra-important to only associate with other "beautiful people." They may also enjoy pointing out physical flaws in others, reaffirming their superiority. *I'm not inviting her to my birthday party because she's fat.*

➤ Children who are frequently given unearned compliments may become emotionally dependent on the approval of others. An emotionally healthy child should be able to accomplish something and immediately feel good about the achievement without having to wait for recognition from others. *Did you see what I did? Wasn't that great?*

(Suggested reading: *The Sneetches,* by Dr. Seuss.)

Reacts badly to feelings of jealousy.

Set an example by admitting when you are jealous of others. Follow up with an explanation of how it is a natural feeling, but you are also happy for that person and hope they will be happy for you some day. Be sure to point out all the wonderful things about your child that might cause others to be envious. And finally, we need to drive home the point that we should try to find out what successful people do so we can do the same things so good things will happen to us too.

(Suggested reading: *The Berenstain Bears and the Green Eyed Monster* by Stan and Jan Berenstain.)

Possesses poor listening skills.

How do you choose your closest friends? If you're like most people, you migrate towards those who listen to whatever it is that you have to say. You want to feel as if someone is interested in you, and will acknowledge that you have feelings and opinions that matter. Good listening skills can work the same kind of magic on budding friendships in kindergarten.

You can encourage attentive listening skills by doing the following:

> ➤ Practice making eye contact when the two of you are talking.
> ➤ Initiate conversations in which you ask for feedback. *How do you feel about that? Do you think that will work? What would you do if you were me?*
> ➤ Point out how when someone changes the subject, or ignores what you've just said, it can hurt your feelings.
> ➤ Work on making appropriate comments by role playing. *Let's say Barbie tells you that she lost her dog. What would you say?*

Is inconsiderate.

Emotionally and physically healthy children become that way due to their parents' devotion when they are small. Unfortunately, some never outgrow the desire to have their expectations met regardless of the cost to others. How can you help your child transition from a total narcissist into a considerate and compassionate human being? Here are some examples of what you can do to encourage the development of empathy, and what you can say to augment the effect of those good intentions as they happen:

> ➤ Let others "go first" in line, even though it is your turn. *We're not in a hurry so let's let these people behind us go first. They're all dressed up so I'm sure they're in a hurry to get somewhere.*
> ➤ You don't have to break out your mop, but clean up after yourself in restaurants and in other public places. *Let's pick up this trash around our table so the waitress won't have so much work to do.*
> ➤ Visit sad and lonely people to brighten their day. *Let's go see how Mrs. Clark is doing after her operation. Maybe there's something we can do for her.*
> ➤ Let another driver have the parking space you wanted. *I'm going to park somewhere else so that woman with all the children in her car won't have so far to walk.*
> ➤ Let your child sign sympathy and get well cards and help think of something nice to say. *Sometimes it will make people feel better if you just say that you're thinking about them.*
> ➤ Don't react badly to poor treatment by a cashier or waitress. *I'll bet she's really tired from working on her feet all day. Poor thing.*

Doesn't seem to have any loyal or regular friends and you can't pinpoint the problem.

Learning to manage rejection is important. We all need to be reminded now and then that no matter what we say or what we do, there will always be someone who doesn't like us. But everyone needs at least one friend. And that one friend usually leads to another and another. The problem is, children typically get so wrapped up in their own loneliness and misery that they don't realize there are a lot of other lonely children out there, just like themselves.

Encourage your child to go on a "search and rescue mission" on the playground.

Step one: Look for someone who looks lonely.
Step two: Smile and say hello.
Step three: Think of something you can do together even if it's just watching someone else play a game.

(Suggested reading: *Hurty Feelings* by Helen Lester, *How to Lose All Your Friends* by Nancy Carlson, *Charlotte's Web* by E.B. White, and *Charlie the Caterpillar* by Dom DeLuise.)

Practice conversation starters.

Hi. My name is Emma. What is your name?
My birthday is September 20th. When is your birthday?
What games do you like to play? Do you want to see my marbles?
What are your favorite cartoons? I like Dora the Explorer.
Do you have any brothers or sisters? I don't have any.
Do you have any pets? I have a cat named Tiger. He likes to sleep on my bed.

Helping Your Child Become More Likeable

First of all, let's take a look at what it means to be "likeable." Is it being a good athlete? Wearing really trendy and expensive clothing? Having perfect features? Easily getting straight A's? Being chosen to sing all the solos in the choir? Or is it having a dad that owns a golf course? Sometimes those things strangely guarantee popularity in school, but not in the beginning. Kindergartners are blind to such advantages and I'm glad. I enjoy listening to them banter back and forth when someone isn't demonstrating proper social graces. They seem to be the only human beings who can do that and then get over it and remain friends.

But as they progress through school, something terrible happens. They stop speaking up and start standing back, hoping that the adults will catch wind of those who are mistreating them and do something about it. Some get tired of waiting and learn dirty tricks to get even with peers they can't stand, and some retreat into their own little worlds trying to avoid being emotionally trampled. Sound familiar?

In my opinion, one of the most important things you can do as a parent is to raise your child's likeability factor. Having friends is one thing, but being "liked" by most people has been touted as being just as important for success as acquiring advanced job skills.[67] More importantly, being an emotionally intelligent child means you're going to have a pretty good shot at becoming a happy adult.

Let's begin by reviewing some of the magnetic traits of people who seem to make and keep friends more easily than others:

➤ Uses good manners.
➤ Practices good hygiene.
➤ Shares and treats others' property with respect.
➤ Is a good listener.
➤ Is aware and respectful of others' personal space.
➤ Can read social cues and respond appropriately.
➤ Does not tattle.
➤ Is considerate and does not bully.
➤ Is not snobbish, self-centered, and can control feelings of jealousy.
➤ Has knowledge of how to join in conversations and activities typical of this age.
➤ Can accept failure and/or losing.

There are some additional ways in which you can realistically raise the bar.

In order to instinctively know how to respond to others, early school-aged children need to be able to imagine how others feel.

Charlie hurt your feelings when he said you have buggy eyes. Teasing hurts, doesn't it? Do you remember how you felt when Tessie didn't want to play with you? That's how Nell will feel if you tell her you don't want to play with her.

Just like adults, children don't have to be all that interesting; they just need to be interested in others and the world around them.

Don't stifle curiosity. The thirst to know new people and experience new things is a trait that can be magnetic. You can be the biggest snore in the world, but people will love you if you are genuinely interested in them or what they are interested in. Resist shooing away any child and instead, fan the flame. Little ones can hold the nails, stir the pot, help choose the best picture to send to grandma, or hand you the copies you've just printed.

Encourage self-discovery.

Kids who can define themselves have more confidence and are less likely to become "invisible" in a group.

I like playing games. My favorite food is grilled cheese. My grandpa is my best friend. I like to read books about animals. I have blond hair like my mom, but I look like my dad.

Emphasize that as strange as it sounds, being able to admit when you're wrong makes people like you better.

It takes bravery to admit when you've told a lie, taken something that belongs to someone else, or made a terrible mistake. The person you've wronged may be mad for a while, but in the long run, it should pay off. Eventually people will learn that you are someone who tells the truth and can be trusted. If nothing else, once the apology is out, you'll feel as if a weight has been lifted from your chest.

(Suggested reading: *Ruthie and the (Not So) Teeny Tiny Lie* by Laura Rankin.)

Label the behavior, not the child.

Don't say, *You are mean.* Say instead, *When you told Cassie that her glasses look stupid, you made her cry. You really hurt her feelings and that was not nice at all. She has to wear glasses so she can see as well as you can. Someday you may have to wear glasses. Wouldn't you feel awful if someone told you that your glasses looked stupid? You need to tell her you're sorry.*

Don't just point out positive behavior; point out the *effect* of the behavior on others.

It's simple. Let's say a woman spills a bag of groceries and the two of you rush to help her. Afterwards, you say, *I think that lady really felt happy that we helped her.*

On the other hand, you should demonstrate the pleasure we should feel when helping others.

I felt really good after we helped that lady. How about you?

(Suggested reading: *Heartprints* by P.K. Hallinan.)

Don't become so over-involved or controlling that you encourage dependency on others.

Intrusive and overbearing parenting can stifle the ability to form independent thoughts and feelings. Over time, children become passive and non-assertive, depending on others to lead the way. People who are clingy can be boring, or at their worst, even downright irritating.

Reinforce the sad fact that no matter what, there will always be someone who doesn't like us. We need to go about our own lives and not worry about it.

Children who are emotionally dependent on the approval of others will often feel hurt and betrayed. Don't try to figure out how to fix it or give it anymore attention than it deserves. Simply acknowledge the hurt and say: *Sometimes people don't like us and we don't know why. It's not your fault, so don't worry about it. Just play with your friends who do like you.*

Help your child feel confident enough to help others.

Emotionally healthy children love to feel helpful. It is up to the adults in their lives to provide opportunities in which they will gain the confidence to step up when others need them. Lower your standards and be creative even when you don't really think that you want any help. For example, it is ridiculous to think that all of your laundry has to be folded to department store perfection. You can't hand over the mower to a five-year old, but any child can "pluck" the grass in areas where you would normally trim with a weed eater. Hyperactive kids love tossing rocks back into the driveway, running up and down stairs to fetch things, and giving shoulder massages. Learn to enjoy having a "side kick."

Model a cheerful attitude.

Tell jokes and silly stories. (*What do cats like to eat for dessert? Mice-cream! What time is it when an elephant sits on a fence? Time to fix the fence! Knock, knock. Who's there? Boo. Boo hoo? Don't cry; it's only a joke!*) Hum, sing, or whistle while you work. Point out what's good about today. (*It's raining? I'll bet there are some ducks out there that are pretty happy about that.*) Greet everyone who comes through the door as if you haven't seen them in years.

(Suggested Reading: *How to Be a Friend: A Guide to Making Friends and Keeping Them* by Laurie Krasny Brown.)

Acquiring a Sense of Responsibility

Even if you could afford a full-time housekeeper, cook, and chauffeur, you wouldn't want to turn your child out into the world not knowing how to be self-sufficient. Most of us work full-time and then make the mistake of coming home and doing everything ourselves. Understandably, we want to save time, avoid messes, have things completed to our standards, and/or we want to baby our children as an expression of love. Many parents do not realize that in doing so, they are projecting the feeling that they view their children as helpless. Every little success boosts self-esteem and nurtures the confidence to try new things and stick with it rather than giving up after the first try.

Children who believe that their parents have faith in their abilities are much happier than those who are treated as if they are guests at a five-star hotel. To get with the program, start lowering your expectations to a reasonable degree and assign age appropriate chores. Emphasize organization and taking proper care of things. If nothing else, children at this age can certainly be expected to do one or more of the following:

> - Help put things away (toys, shoes, magazines), and throw away trash.
> - Carry dirty dishes to the sink.
> - Make beds. (Use comforters instead of bed spreads.)
> - Gather up dirty clothes and towels and carry them to the laundry room.
> - Feed and water pets.
> - Dust with chemical-free cloths. (Dusting books and lining them up according to size is strangely an enjoyable activity for many children at this age.)
> - Set the table. (Resist the urge to straighten utensils, etc. If they are in the right place, leave them alone.)

Getting cooperation is easier if you empower your child by giving him or her "choices" that have consequences.

Here are some examples of what you might say:

Would you rather watch cartoons on Saturday morning and then dust the living room afterwards, or would you like to dust the living room in the morning, and then go to Jessie's house to play in the afternoon?

As soon as you feed the cat, I'll fix your breakfast.

After you put your dirty clothes in the laundry basket, I'll get your play dough out for you.

Don't undermine the teacher.

Whatever the teacher decides, you need to go with it. Children who grow up thinking they can weasel their way out of tough situations are bound to develop a weak work ethic and will be more likely to have problems with interpersonal relationships.

Don't give empty praise.

Be specific when you can. It will reinforce good behavior.

You did a great job cleaning off the table. You were careful not to throw away any silverware, you stacked all the plates up, and you wiped every spot off of the table.

You did a nice job on your homework. You took your time tracing your letters so your paper looks very neat.

Praise effort as well as results.

It is important to feel as if we are making progress even when we fail. It is also important to learn that not all efforts end in rewards or victories. We can't give up and allow someone else to take over for us. Persistence is vital for success.

You are working really hard. I'm proud of you. It takes a lot of practice to learn to print.

From the first day of school and on, it is imperative that you insist that every assignment be completed.

Some parents tend not to worry as long as their child seems intelligent. Time after time, I've cringed at meetings during which the teacher is exasperated because a student won't complete assigned tasks, and the parents fail to see the problem. Some actually rationalize that the child can read, is a whiz at math, and seems to be able to perform academic circus tricks, so why should it matter?

The point of completing all assignments even when you're academically up to speed is three-fold:

> Children need to learn to be responsible for meeting the expectations of teachers (and bosses).
> Once you've instilled a good work ethic, it will carry over into other areas of your child's life.
> Eventually the "whiz kid" effect will fizzle out when academic success requires more than a basic foundation of knowledge.

When you say…

My child is bored. That is why he/she won't do the work. You're not making the class challenging enough.

The teacher thinks…

Please. Why would I try to come up with more challenging assignments when your child won't do anything to begin with?

Whether brilliant, average, or slow, children are often "bored" in school.

Should you offer incentives for good grades?

Some kids are naturally hard-wired to work hard to avoid punishment, some will work for rewards, and some need both to stay motivated. Hopefully you'll never have to worry about utilizing either, but "never say never."

The Value of Homework

One of your most important responsibilities as a parent is to monitor and help with homework. Don't discount it as just something else that has to be done. Teachers do not concoct assignments to torture parents; they do it for three sound reasons:

> ➤ To help students retain information longer by repeating what was covered in class.
> ➤ To increase the understanding of material through additional problems, reading assignments, or projects.
> ➤ To give troubled students the opportunity to "catch up" on important skills.

If you get tired of monitoring or tutoring your child night after night (and eventually you will), remember this:

Your child would rather be doing something else too!

Work through your urges to give up, let it go, or say *never mind*. In fact, it is a good idea to admit that you don't really want to sit down and work either. Then you can model consistency and self-discipline by saying:

Let's work really hard and get this done, and then we can have some fun.

At times, it will take enormous discipline for you to stay the course, but do not waver. This is where it all begins. This is your first shot at encouraging the development of good work habits, which in turn will nurture an independent little worker who will learn to enjoy the satisfying sense of accomplishment. Even though you might have to put up with a little whining, consistently following through with homework also creates a comforting sense of security. (*I can trust my parents to always make me do the right things.*)

What if the work seems too easy?

If the assignment appears to be a waste of time, something that a simpleton could do, then you should feel proud. Some students *can't* do it, so be thankful for the affirmation that your child is on track.

You can make just about any assignment more challenging and/or more interesting by adding your own twist. (*Let's see if you can count backwards from 10! Let's see if we can think of more words that begin with "g!" I wonder what kind of dog this is. There are different kinds of dogs. They call them breeds. There are beagles, huskies, boxers, and lots of other kinds. Let's look at some pictures on the Internet and see if we can find out what breed this dog is.*)

You can also have some fun by having your child pretend to be the teacher, explain the assignment to you, and then "help" you complete the work. You will learn loads about the teacher's classroom management style and teaching techniques through what I'm sure will be a delightful imitation.

Mastery of the work at this level also means that you don't have to monitor every second of every assignment. The ultimate goal for every student is to become a self-propelled learner, so there you go. You should be nearby and supportive, yet have the freedom to go about your own business.

What if the assignment(s) appears to be "busy work?"

Don't knock it. If you do, your child will sense your lack of faith in the teacher's abilities and may not learn to respect authority. You can always ask the teacher about the value of such an assignment, but don't be surprised if you feel a little silly for having done so. All homework has some relevance, even if it is meant to merely further develop fine motor skills, a necessary prelude to being able to print legibly.

An example would be an assignment sheet with the instructions to "color all the fish blue, the birds red, and the kittens yellow." The cognitive benefits include reinforcement of the ability to identify primary colors and practice in visually discriminating different shapes. If nothing else, it is yet another chance to improve fine motor skills, as long as you encourage staying within the lines and using even strokes for more uniform shading. Coloring may seem like a worthless activity, but it is a precursor to developing neat and fluid handwriting by helping one gain control over his or her dominant hand. Every simple task completed will help a child process and connect future information more easily.

If you are not satisfied to sit idly by, then you can supplement the lesson with your own ideas. You might ask, *Do you know what kind of birds are red?*

What kind of fish have you seen? Do you think blue fish really exist? Do you know where dolphins live? Do you think Grandpa has dolphins in his pond? What other colors could a kitten be? Where do birds go in the wintertime?

It is important to keep pushing just a little more and a little longer in all of his or her pursuits. Working past the point of boredom or fatigue is the key to developing self-control, strength of will, diligence, self-reliance, and responsibility.

What do you do about a whiner who can't seem to get started?

First, let's think positively. Don't confuse a procrastinator with someone who just doesn't know how or where to begin. If you have to demonstrate how to go at it, don't worry about it. That's what teachers have to do every single day with the majority of students.

If you're dealing with a daydreamer, a dawdler, or a stubborn mule, then you'll just have to monitor every assignment until your child takes the initiative to work independently.

> ➤ Stick to a set time to sit down and begin.
> ➤ Don't ever say anything that might give the impression that homework is an optional activity.
> ➤ Never utilize homework time as a form of punishment.
> ➤ Don't tolerate excuses to get up and down from his or her seat.
> ➤ Leave the most pleasant task for last, especially if you enjoy reading together. When everything else is completed, you can move away from your work area and cuddle up in a comfy chair together.

(Suggested reading: *The Berenstain Bears and the Homework Hassle* by Stan Berestain and Jan Berenstain.)

What should you do if the work seems too difficult?

Resist the temptation to do the work yourself. Homework is more than a learning tool for students; it is also a means for teachers to evaluate their own effectiveness. If everything looks hunky-dory, then it only gives the false impression that the material has been adequately covered and the teacher should move on to the next thing.

An occasional rough spot is nothing to become alarmed about. Sometimes kids do not feel well, they're tired, they're upset about something, or they just flat out don't pay attention in class and miss the information needed to do an outside assignment. All you have to do is jump in and "re-teach" the information. Kindergartners shouldn't have homework that normally takes any longer than 20 minutes to complete, so taking a little longer to catch up will be worth the effort for peace of mind for the both of you.

What if you've clearly made a mistake in sending your child to school too early?

If homework becomes a constant nightmare, then you need to take action. First meet with the teacher to discuss the problem and possible solutions. Chances are, the teacher will be well aware of what might be wrong before you make contact. (Refer to the section entitled *Straight Talk about Special Education.*)

What if you're lucky enough to have a natural-born, self-directed learner that doesn't need your help?

You still need to check out everything that travels back and forth so you won't miss any communications intended for you. You also need to show that you are interested and excited about what is going on at school.

If your normally self-sufficient child suddenly stops doing homework or feigns ignorance, it may be an attention-seeking streak so you will spend more time together. To stay on top of it all, make sitting down together a part of your daily routine. Once you've checked for information intended for you, then busy yourself with something constructive to improve your own life. Pay bills, catch up on correspondence, model reading for pleasure, demonstrate lifelong learning by researching something interesting, start a new hobby, take on a project, plan a trip, or take an online class.

Other Homework Tips

➢ The very first thing you should do is look through every compartment of the backpack for notes, newsletters, and assignments from the teacher. This will also clue you in as to whether or not fees and lunch money are making it into the right hands. (If you happen to be a parent of twins, I am an advocate for keeping them in the same class so you'll have an easier time keeping everything straight.)

➢ Children thrive on routine, familiarity, and consistency. Even though you may become bored out of your gourd, stick with your setup for completing homework. Eventually it will become habitual and you won't have to nag anymore.

➢ Don't set up shop in front of the TV. You'll be inviting distractions and setting an insincere tone about the importance of homework. Later on, when your child matures enough to complete homework without supervision, it doesn't matter where it is done if it is done well.

➤ Utilize motivational tools. Make math practice more fun by using M&M's, Fruit Loops, or other tasty treats as manipulatives. If you have to redo several problems, don't "hide the evidence." The teacher needs to see what students aren't getting to be sure the material is being sufficiently covered in class.

➤ Prove that persistence pays off by placing a penny in a see-through container for every correct answer when practicing any type of repetitive work. When the container is full, go to the bank together to cash in the coins for spending money.

➤ Display good work on your refrigerator, family bulletin board, or on your child's bedroom door to demonstrate your support.

➤ There is no rule against enlisting the help of other people, such as grandparents, to help with homework. Parent involvement is best, but if you are not always available, make sure that someone is taking your place. Even if you have to pay a high school student or older sibling to "tutor," it will be worth it in the long run.

➤ The more in tune you are with what is happening at school, the more secure your child will feel. It doesn't matter who monitors homework, as long as you make a point to look through everything and make positive comments about what is being learned.

➤ Keep all doubt out of your voice about the length, difficulty, or purpose of any assignment. If you think it is that big of a deal, call the teacher in private.

➤ Purchase a globe, map of the world, or an atlas to do some exploring whenever a story or assignment refers to an unfamiliar place. Improve critical thinking skills by asking, *How could we get there? Could we drive? How long do you think the trip would take? What do you suppose the weather is like this time of year?*

➤ As your child progresses in school and you begin to sense what subjects are bound to be challenging, start looking for supplemental books, games, and tools to use at home that look appealing.

➤ Always read the directions. This is another good habit that you can easily reinforce. In addition to homework assignments, read aloud the directions to everything—recipes, cleaning products, shampoo, etc. You may, of course, invent your own shortened version.

➤ Don't attempt to micro-manage homework. Instead, encourage self-sufficiency. This will cultivate a sense of independence and responsibility. (*See! I did it all by myself!*)

> It is never too early to begin teaching good study skills. A good rule to begin with is: *Do the easy parts first, and then go back to the hard things that will take more time.*

> Don't ever say, *You don't have any homework? Great!* Ingrain the habit of doing something worthwhile every night by keeping books or learning games around to fill in your regular time slot for homework. Instead, say, *You don't have any homework? Great! We can play a math game or read together. Which would you prefer?*

> Again, never ever use homework time as a punishment.

Scoring Points with the School Secretaries

In my opinion, these women have the most thankless jobs in a school system. Their heads are usually spinning with an avalanche of paperwork, ringing phones, demanding office traffic, and other monotonous tasks for which they are paid little more than circus peanuts. In spite of this, they are the very people that will drop everything and help you in a pinch. They have been known to search backpacks for lost car keys and spy on students who were boo-hooing on their way out the door in the morning.

Follow these suggestions, and I can guarantee there won't be any eye rolling when they see you coming, and you will have a dependable support system when you need one.

> ➤ Do not direct your anger about school issues at them. They cannot do anything about incompetent teachers or a lice epidemic. They are not responsible for calling off school during inclement weather. They do not make the decision to raise lunch prices, nor do they choose the "student of the grading period." Ask them to direct you to the appropriate person before you blow.
> ➤ If your child will be absent, immediately call the school so they will not have to add you to their long list of negligent parents they have to track down.
> ➤ Don't drop a tardy child off at the curb. Park your car and enter the main office and follow the procedure for signing in late. The secretary responsible for recording attendance has better things to do than "guess" when your child arrived, or go back and change a recorded absence to a tardy.
> ➤ If you have an appointment during the day, send a note that morning. Make every effort to limit the number of times you pull your child

out of school, and make sure it is for a legitimate reason and not just to beat after-school traffic. This interrupts your child's education, the entire class, and adds to a secretary's pile of paperwork.

➢ Do not make a habit of calling to say that you've had a change of plans and you need your child to ride another bus, go to grandma's, etc. If you have an emergency situation, they will be glad to help you, but a fleeting decision to take off for the mall will elicit little sympathy.

➢ Never call and ask a secretary to catch a child before he or she gets on the bus. The end of the day is chaotic enough without someone foolishly believing that a secretary would be able to leave the office and chase down a school bus.

➢ Do not call the school to find out what's for lunch, when Christmas vacation begins, or anything else of a trivial nature. Hang up the calendars, lunch menus, and newsletters that are sent home, and keep the school website bookmarked for easy reference.

➢ Follow directions for turning in fees, picture money, etc., to a tee. If the directions say to send a check or money order, then don't send cash. If you've received a notice to return school photos that you don't want to purchase, then do it right away. Again, these are problems that will mentally stamp you as negligent or a pest. Incidentally, after the secretaries get tired of hunting you down, they will place a record of money owed in your child's file. Keep all receipts in your "central command station" for easy retrieval.

➢ Only in the case of an extreme emergency should you ever call the school and ask to speak to your child. If you do, an administrator will more than likely want to speak to you first to be sure the reason warrants interrupting a class.

➢ Don't be "one of those people" who call the school, hear the sound of a friendly voice, and forget that you are talking to a secretary and not a psychotherapist. They are entirely too busy to listen to the microscopic details of your personal life. Besides, over the years, "all of those people" become one voice, one family, and one story, so look for another outlet if you want to be taken seriously.

➢ Please try to send a token of appreciation at least once during the year for the selfless service that these women provide. If you can imagine the germs that collect on their doorknobs and phones, you'll know that even a single container of anti-bacterial wipes or a box of anti-viral tissues will have them grinning from ear to ear.

For Moms Who are Going Back to Work

As soon as you've made the decision to return to work, start talking about how excited you are. You will also be learning new things, making new friends, and getting some new clothes. It doesn't matter how tired or discouraged you become; you can solve a host of potential problems for a kindergartner if you at least pretend to be enamored with your new adventure. Maybe you'll both "catch the fever."

Here are some other tips:

State in simple language what going to work will mean.

> ➤ *While you're at school, Mommy will get to go to work.*
> ➤ *Mommy will be making money to help buy new things like school clothes for you and a mower for Daddy!*
> ➤ *We'll be able to go out to eat more often and we'll even get to go to the movies!*

Develop a strong network of people who can help you out when your child is sick or needs something.

This is ultra-important if you are taking an inflexible position. You'll need people to step in when your child is sick or needs forgotten items delivered to the school. You should also find people who can attend school events such as plays or awards assemblies so your child will not feel orphaned. Don't forget to enlist the help of aunts, uncles, grandparents, neighbors, close family friends, babysitters, and even your church family.

When is the best time to go back to work or start a new job?

Only you can answer this for yourself. Unfortunately, you may not have a choice if an employer dictates your starting date. If you return before school begins, you'll have a chance to get used to your own routine before adding homework and other school-related responsibilities to your schedule. If you wait until after school begins, then you can get the school-related stuff worked out before you have to start pulling on panty hose again.

Explain that just because you come home dog tired doesn't mean you don't like it.

You probably won't be the only one who will come home whining when exhausted. Say that you know how it feels, but once you're both rested up, tomorrow will be a new day! Then take care of business, such as supper and homework, cuddle up in a chair and read together to relax, and then go to bed early.

(Suggested reading: *When Momma Comes Home* by Eileen Spinelli.)

Keep working out the kinks.

If you still want home cooked meals but you're too exhausted to cook, then cook several dishes on your day off to microwave and/or freeze for busy evenings.

If you want some play time together instead of being a slave to homework assignments, then ask your after-school caregiver to monitor the work.

Stop taking on every responsibility. You should never have to pick up toys or books (quarantine them if you do), hang up coats, put away shoes, make beds, or pick up dirty clothes.

Be ingenious in fighting the chaos. The size of your purse has probably grown considerably since the last time you went to work. Having more and deeper compartments only means that you will be digging longer for what you are looking for. Compartmentalize everything into clear zip-lock bags. Place cosmetics in one, checkbook, billfold, ink pens and notepad in another, etc., and then you can lift them out to find the one you're looking for.

Utilize your "central command station" to stay organized for work, and lay out your clothing the night before.

Don't let guilt eat you up.

Stay-at-home moms may be accessible all day long, but what really counts is direct and focused contact. Meals, homework, and other rituals are more than sufficient to fulfill that need.

Share your world with your child.

It amazes me how many of my students have no idea what their parents do at work. Talking about your responsibilities and what you like and don't like can be educational on many levels. You can also use your daily experiences to initiate a running dialog about what is going on in school.

(Suggested reading: *The Berenstain Bears and Mama's New Job* by Stan Berenstain and Jan Berenstain.)

Ways to Keep a Broken Marriage from Breaking Your Child

Children are the center of their own universe. When they are too young to understand cause and effect, they often believe they are somehow directly responsible for everything that happens. Unfortunately, this includes their parents splitting up. There are ways to lessen the trauma of divorce, which will in turn lessen problems in school.

(Suggested reading: *I Don't Want to Talk about It* by Jeanie Franz Ransom, or *Dinosaurs Divorce* by Marc Brown and Laurie Krasney Brown)

Do not deny that you are having problems.

Children can sense negative vibes between parents, and may worry excessively. Don't sugar coat anything, but be reassuring. It is important that you repeatedly say, *You did not cause this, and you cannot fix it.*

Don't ever say that you are not in love anymore.

This is terrifying to a five- or six-year old who may interpret this to mean that someday you may also stop loving him or her too.

Continue to maintain schedules and rituals.

Talk about any changes that have to be made. A sense of order will help diminish the "fear of the unknown" and create feelings of comfort and stability as opposed to disappointment and abandonment. Do not allow your grief to interfere with you going to work or your child going to school. It is daily routines and mundane chores, including homework, that help stabilize topsy-turvy feelings no matter how old you are.

(Suggested reading: *Good-Bye, Daddy!* by Brigette Weninger.)

Do not "drop by" the school for a visit.

School is commonly a sanctuary for students facing stress at home so don't take that away. If something is wrong, let us know and we'll dole out additional attention if needed. Our aim is to nurture children so we can educate them. If we need you, we'll let you know.

Keep your focus on school success.

Some parents don't realize how resilient their children are and make the mistake of suggesting how miserable they ought to be. Don't dwell on the negative aspects of your failed marriage, especially about spending time apart. Sure, Daddy or Mommy are missed, but stay upbeat about upcoming visitations, and never limit phone calls with an estranged parent because of your insecurities, jealousy, or anger.

If you happen to be the absent one, here are some suggestions for starting a conversation about school when you call:

> *What is your teacher like?*
> *Did you do anything new today?*
> *What is the hardest thing you had to do?*
> *Who do you play with at recess?*
> *What do you like to play?*
> *Did you read any good stories today?*
> *Did anything funny happen today?*
> *Who are your best friends and what are they like?*
> *What do you like the most about school?*

Maintaining a cooperative attitude about school is a continuous opportunity to help improve your relationship with your ex-spouse.

Be willing to help with scheduling transportation, completing homework, or coming up with needed supplies.

Keep appropriate school staff apprised of any developments or changes in the stability of your home life.

The school counselor and regular classroom teacher is a good place to start. They will in turn notify appropriate employees of any developments. Please understand that you cannot stop an estranged spouse from doing anything unless you have a court document designating you as the "residential" or "custodial" parent. Until you have delivered this document to the school, both parents still have equal rights. The only exception would be an official document from your local children's protective agency or a restraining order.

Hopefully there won't be any monkey business on either party's part. Children thrive on a sense of normalcy, so school may be the one and only place to escape their emotional pain. You can call and check to see if there are any signs of trauma, but let staff members deal with it on their own. Do not visit the school to intervene.

Don't put the teacher or any other school employees in the middle of your disputes.

Don't ask us to "let you know" if your ex-spouse does this or says that. If a parent is out of line in any way, we will address the situation in the manner in which we are professionally trained.

Don't unload all your complaints about your "ex" on us.

There are two sides to every story and children and school employees do not need to know either one. No matter how hard it is, please reserve your anger for your personal adult support system. We only need to be aware of substantiated information about the mental or physical abuse of your children. If we believe that something has happened, be assured that we will be on high alert to look for evidence to report to authorities. We are required by law to do so.

Do not allow your problems to bleed into your child's life.

A sweet little girl once revealed to me: *Daddy cheated on Mommy and me.* The point being, kids will typically feel they've done something to cause the split. Don't fuel the fire by detailing who is at fault.

(Suggested reading: *It's Not Your Fault, Koko Bear: A Read Together Book for Parents and Young Children During Divorce* by Vicki Lansky.)

Don't fight for custody, or even visitation rights, if you are planning on leaving your child with a babysitter or someone else most of the time.

Please weigh your decisions carefully. Having your parents separate is a traumatic event that requires additional attention from parents, not less. Bitterness and child support payments can sometimes cloud one's judgment. Will you be available to keep up with the day-to-day demands of a school-aged child? No child wants to be passed off to your stand-in, and the same goes for us. School employees have to be careful about the legalities of dealing with anyone who is not a biological parent.

Both parents should attend school activities and conferences *together.*

You don't have to arrive together, but you have no idea the impact a united front can make if you can attend functions and sit side by side. If you can get along (even if you are faking it), you are demonstrating the true spirit of good parenting. Strive to promote an atmosphere in which your child perceives, "The adults in my life all agree."

You can alleviate some of the stress of having to be together by keeping the focus on your child. You need to support one another on problems and solutions and this is the perfect opportunity to do so. For instance, if a "time out chair" works for you, then share this information.

Don't invite trouble.

Leave your girlfriend, boyfriend, relatives, and close friends home until you work out all the awkwardness in your new situation. Custodial parents have the right, according to the Family Educational Rights and Family Act, to ban "other parties" from attending parent/teacher conferences, as well as preventing them from signing kids out of school or obtaining student information. In 2004, this law was interpreted to include spouses of non-custodial parents. Additionally, it was determined that a step-parent must be in the home on a day-to-day basis, and must be acting on behalf of a custodial parent who is "absent" (at work, in the hospital, etc.), in order to act in his or her capacity concerning school matters.[68] Whether you are the custodial parent or just a biological parent, you should make every effort to deal with the school directly, and not through any type of "messenger."

If you and your "ex" cannot get along, then attend conferences and activities anyway and sit far apart. Non-custodial parents have the right to do so unless there is a restraining order that specifies otherwise.

Non-custodial parents have the right to view school records, request a parent-teacher conference, and attend school activities unless specifically prohibited from doing so by a court of law.[69]

It would be great if your ex-spouse would cheerfully provide you with grade cards and school newsletters, but we realize that even if you are getting along famously, this chore has the potential to cause friction between the two of you. Once you've missed an open house or holiday program, you'll probably always wonder if you're missing something else.

Thanks to the Family Education Rights and Privacy Act, even if you are not the custodial parent, you have a right to school information. The law doesn't require that schools mail this information unless you live far enough away that you can't drop by to pick it up yourself. Schools also have the right to charge you for copies and postage, but may not. Your best bet is to provide the school secretaries with pre-addressed, stamped envelopes for their convenience. (Some schools require that you do this anyway.) Find out how often grade cards and newsletters are produced and match that number.

Sometimes non-custodial parents mistakenly believe that their ex-spouse or school employees have not been forthcoming with information when it has been printed in the local newspaper for any interested party to see. If you live in another community, you should locate and subscribe to the newspaper that generally covers your child's school.

Another way to make sure that you do not miss anything is to attend parent-teacher organization meetings. This group is at the hub of all school activities. If you are reluctant to attend because you are male, let me encourage you by telling you that female members are usually giddy at the sight of any new member, especially one who can lug boxes and climb ladders with ease.

If you are a step-parent, be a champion one.

If you really want to be accepted and loved by a step-child, then you must always treat the absent parent with respect. Never say anything derogatory or play any kind of "head games" to try and prove that you are superior in any way. I once met a woman who gave her step-daughter two kisses at bedtime—one from herself, and one from the little girl's mother. Another nice idea would be to ask the estranged parent to record a bedtime story or prayer that you can play each night.

(Suggested reading: *The Family Book* by Todd Parr, or *Two Homes* by Claire Masurel,)

Homemade Fun for Overachieving Parents

I've always admired people who are willing to risk their sanity and the condition of their kitchens to make their children happy. So if you're one of those people, then here they are—recipes honed by my friends for making a mess of fun.

Watercolor Paint

Supplies:

> - 4 tablespoons of baking soda
> - 2 tablespoons of white vinegar
> - 1/2 teaspoon of glycerin
> - 2 tablespoons of cornstarch
> - food coloring

Directions:

Mix the vinegar and baking soda until it stops foaming. Add the glycerin and cornstarch and mix thoroughly. Pour the mixture into individual containers before adding food coloring or you'll be stuck with only one color. Let paint "set" overnight.

Finger Paint

Supplies:

> - ½ cup cornstarch
> - 3 tablespoons of sugar
> - ½ teaspoon of salt
> - food coloring

Directions:

Stir the cornstarch, sugar, and salt in a saucepan over low heat for about 10 to 15 minutes. Once that mixture has thickened, remove from heat and allow it to cool. Pour into separate containers before mixing in the food coloring if you would like more than one color.

Play Dough

Supplies:

- ➢ 1 cup water
- ➢ 1 cup flour
- ➢ ½ cup salt
- ➢ 2 teaspoons of cream of tarter
- ➢ 2 teaspoons cooking oil
- ➢ food coloring

Directions:

Combine ingredients in a saucepan. Cook and stir with a wooden spoon until it reaches a kneading consistency. Remove it and work it with your hands for two minutes. Store in an airtight container or sealable bag so it will remain soft.

Paper Mache

You can use this recipe to make piñatas or sculptures.

Supplies:

- ➢ 3 cups warm water
- ➢ 2 cups of plain flour
- ➢ a pinch of salt
- ➢ materials to build a "form"
- ➢ drop clothes and old clothes

Directions:

Before you begin preparing the paste, you need to build a "form." Use masking or duct tape and cardboard, cereal boxes, chicken wire, balls, wrapping paper tubes, balloons, or just about anything to create the shape you want to cover.

If you are making a piñata, use a balloon for the main part of your form, leaving a small space open at the top when adding strips. Once the form is dry, pop the balloon and pull it out through the hole. Use the hole to fill with candy and/or small toys along with some tissue paper so it won't be too heavy to hang. Poke two additional holes in the top to thread kite string through. Be careful not to make your layers too thick in order to cut down on additional weight.

Mix the water, flour, and salt until pasty. (The salt will prevent mold if you plan to keep your creation for a while.) Work the paste with your hands to remove lumps. The consistency should feel somewhat like pancake batter.

Tear, don't cut, strips of newspaper to dip into the mixture to cover your form. As you dip each strip, use your fingers like a squeegee to remove excess paste. Smooth the wet strips over your form, overlapping if necessary to cover the entire shape for a uniform look.

Let your project dry for at least 24 hours before painting and/or adding artistic touches such as cotton balls, feathers, glitter, etc.

Homemade Butter

Supplies:

> ➤ heavy cream
> ➤ a glass jar with a lid

Directions:

Fill a glass jar ¾ full of heavy cream. Use baby food jars for small portions, and peanut butter jars or pickle jars for larger portions. Start with smaller sized jars until you can judge how long it takes for butter to form.

Simply take turns shaking the jar until butter has formed around the edges. Pour out any remaining liquid before using or refrigerating. The leftover liquid is actually buttermilk, so you can use it for baking if you'd like.

When I was a Brownie Scout, we would recite the following English nursery rhyme while rolling a giant jar from person to person in a "cherry pie circle" on the floor:

Come butter come,
Come butter come.
Peter standing at the gate,
Waiting for his buttered cake.
Come butter come!

How Do You Know if You are Doing the Right Things?

The most common question I hear during the screening process is:

What exactly should I be doing to prepare my child for kindergarten?

The following list is comprised of suggestions to give you an idea of what parents of many of my accomplished and well-adjusted students believe made a difference. The wonderful news about all this is that most parents were also of the opinion that you don't really have to sweat bullets to be good at this. Their suggestions can easily be put into practice just by making sure that resources and opportunities are there for the taking, and by exercising more patience when verbally interacting. Better yet, they feel you shouldn't shoulder the entire burden of providing meaningful and enjoyable activities. You should enlist neighbors, relatives, and anyone else interested in your child for help. For example, do you have a son who needs to develop a little more coordination and become more physically active? Hire a physically fit male role model to babysit instead of a female and tell him what you want him to accomplish.

Nevertheless, here is a list of things that other parents have done to encourage the development of skills that are crucial not only for school, but for life in general.

> ➤ Provide lots of play things that will develop hand control, especially the dominant hand, such as play dough, puzzles, crayons, and pencils. Look for coloring books that include picture captions and workbooks that include activities such as copying the letters of the alphabet. The key thing to remember is that you should provide these

items but not insist they be used. Kids will show an avid interest when they are cognitively ready.

➤ Read together everyday, even if you can only squeeze in a bedtime story.

➤ Be verbally engaging. Do it in the car, at mealtime, or whenever you're together and it's not necessary that you focus on something or someone else. If you think your child is boring, it's because you haven't challenged his or her sense of wonder or taken the time to really listen to his or her ideas and opinions. Conversing is also conducive for the acquisition of a larger vocabulary, development of the ability to express one's self, and for honing listening skills.

➤ Running errands together is potentially developmental on several levels. Again, you can engage in stimulating conversations in transit. This will nurture a better understanding of the outside world and how everything and everyone interconnects. He or she will be exposed to other people, some of whom will be nice and engaging, and others who won't be so nice. This is an opportunity to model how to deal with crabby people and then "shake it off," a very important lesson in not letting others control your emotions. And finally, it will be great practice in learning manners, patience, and appropriate behavior in public.

➤ Help identify things that are real as opposed to things that are make believe, except of course for Santa Claus, the Tooth Fairy, and the Easter Bunny. Let them fizzle out on their own.

➤ When you send cards or gifts from your family, work on having your child print his or her own name for practice, to help eliminate self-centeredness, and to reinforce the comforting feeling of being part of a strong family unit.

➤ Point out people in positions of authority and what they do. (Firefighters, policemen, military personnel, the mayor, the post master, etc.)

➤ Demonstrate how we use numbers. Ask for help in counting items, checking the temperature, measuring with cooking tools, checking gauges, and estimating sizes.

➤ Resist doing everything around the house yourself. Kids like to feel as if they're part of the hub of a family.

➤ Allow playtime on the computer, within limits of course. Too much time looking at any screen cuts into other developmental areas. The benefits include learning to control a mouse, developing fine motor skills in the dominant hand, and the limitless possibilities for strengthening pre-academic skills. Rather than purchasing software that will be outgrown quickly, search online for free interactive sites that are geared for pre-school and kindergarten students.

➤ Encourage and provide the opportunities for creative and physical play rather than settling for a quiet child slumped in front of the TV.

➤ Find ways to include your child in your own pursuits. If you like to scrapbook, provide some materials, your cast-off pictures, and a separate book to fill. If you are a gardener, provide some child-sized tools and some plants to tend. Whatever you do, vow to get over the extra mess. Learning to explore interesting things can be a deterrent later on for getting bored and exploring drugs, alcohol, and sex. Besides, someday you'll miss the company.

➤ Don't avoid restaurants, church services, movie theatres and other places that require sitting still and being quiet. This doesn't mean that you can't remove your child when he or she becomes mutinous; it just means that you need to keep working on encouraging self-control. Some kids are stubborn and hard to manage, but this skill will not magically develop by itself. You need to work at it.

➤ Do not make every insignificant decision. Offer some safe choices so he or she will learn to weigh possible consequences and feel more confident in his or her own abilities. Start with a simple menu that may please the rest of the family, and go from there. You may end up on the vacation of a lifetime. Thomas the Train may not be real, but I found out that Amtrak is the next best thing.

The Best History Book Your Child Will Ever Read

Think how wonderful it would have been if your parents had kept a journal of your experiences when you were too young for those unique memories to imprint themselves permanently on your brain. You would not only be able to get a glimpse of what your life was like, you would also get a clearer sense of what your parents were feeling.

You don't have to write volumes, or even every day; just record the things you find yourself smiling about.

September 10th—You told me you loved Mrs. Johnson, which was bittersweet to hear. I wanted your teacher to love you, but I wasn't quite ready for someone else to steal your affection.

September 14th—You came home with dried, dirty tear streaks down your cheeks and a Band-aide on your chin. You said you pushed Paris because she took your ball, and then she pushed you back harder and you fell down. You both have to miss recess tomorrow. I asked you what you learned from this and you said, "I'm not gonna play with Paris or marry her!"

September 20th—You had a substitute teacher today. I asked you what her name was and you said, "I forget, but it was really loud in our room." You also said Mr. Newton, your principal, kept peeking in the door. I asked you why and you said, "I don't know, but I waved at him and he waved at me!" You also said that "Mrs. Johnson teaches a whole lot better. They should pay her."

October 1st—I bought you a pair of Ohio State Buckeye socks and I already know that you are going to want to wear them every single day of your life. I'll probably wash them out in the bathroom sink and hang them over the register to dry every night until they wear out.

A Final Note

Whatever you do, enjoy the ride. After all, you will get to dabble in all those things you loved as a kid—reading books with really cool pictures, messing around with scissors and paste, drawing and coloring, singing silly songs, and skipping down the street just for the heck of it.

This could be your last chance to get away with having this kind of fun—until you become a grandparent!

Notes

1. Social Security Online, The Official Website of the U.S. Social Security Administration, *Your Social Security Number and Card,* www.ssa.gov/ssnumber/.

2. Mexican American Legal Defense and Education Fund, MALDEF Federal Education Rights Pamphlet, *Know Your K-12 Education Rights: The Federal Education Rights of Students and Their Families,* 2008.

3. Minnesota Department of Health, *Changing (Amending) a Birth Record,* www.health.state.mn.us/divs/chs/osr/amend.html.

4. Legal Services Organization, South Arizona Legal Aid, Inc., *How to Change Your Name,* www.azlawhelp.org/articles_info.cfm?mc=1&sc=8&articleid=60.

5. Chris Kueny-Rongione, "Torture Your Children-Hyphenate Name: One Man's Epic Struggle with a Complicated Surname," *The Berkeley Beacon.com,* 24 April 2003, available at www.media.berkeleybeacom. com/media/storage/paper169/news/2003/04/24/Opinion/Torture.Your. ChildHyphenate.Name-425737.shtml.

6. Robert T. Baker and Kimball H. Carey of Means, Bichimer, Burkholder & Baker Co., L.P.A., *Baker's Ohio School Law Guide, Volume 1,* (Cincinnati: Anderson Publishing Co., 2000), Section 9.01, 468.

7. It is very rare for any school—private, chartered, or public—to not receive some kind of federal program funding. Title 1 funds for reading and math intervention are one such example.

8. U.S. Department of Education, *Family Educational Rights and Privacy Act (FERPA),* www.ed.gov/policy/gen/guid/fpco/ferpa/index.html.

9. Wendy Craycraft, *Is There a Relation Between Age of Kindergarten Enrollment and Academic Success?* Muskingum College, 2002, 43.

10. Wrightslaw.com, *Full text of the No Child Left Behind Act; Analysis, Interpretation, and Commentary,* www.wrightslaw.com/nclb/.

11. Southwest Educational Development Laboratory, Classroom Compass, Volume 3, Number 2, *How Can Research on the Brain Inform Education?* www.sedl.org/scimath/compass/v03n02/1.html.

12. Dr. James Dobson, Focus on the Family, *How would being a late bloomer and having trouble learning to read be related?* www.family.custhelp.com/cgi-bin/family.cfg/php/enduser/sti_adp?p_faqid=805.

13. Kathy Hirsh-Pasek, PH.D., and Roberta MichnickGolinkoff, PH.D., Buzzle.com, Intelligent Life on the Web, *How Our Children Really Learn and Why They Need to Play More and Memorize Less,* www.buzzle.com/editorials/10-4-2003-46152.asp.

14. Education Commission of the States, ECS Education Policy Issue Site: Kindergarten, www.ecs.org/html/Issue.asp?issueID=77.

15. The National Institute on Deafness and Other Communication Disorders, *Hearing, Ear Infections, and Deafness,*www.nicdc.nih.gov/health/hearing/.

16. Wayne Steedman, Esq., Wrightslaw.com, *10 Tips: How to Use IDEA 2004 to Improve Your Child's Special Education,* www.wrightslaw.com/idea/art/10.tips.steedman.htm.

17. (Dobson, Focus on the Family.)

18. American Optometric Association, *Comprehensive Eye and Vision Examination,* www.aoa.org/eye-exams.xml.

19. (Wrightslaw.com, *No Child Left Behind.*)

20. Allan S. Bloom and Others, "A Comparison of the Stanford-Binet Abbreviated and Complete Forms for Developmentally Disabled Children," *Journal of Clinical Psychology*, April 1977, 477-80.

21. Increase Brain Power.com, *IQ Scale,* www.increasebrainpower.com/iq-scale.html.

22. New York State Office of Children and Family Services, *Say No! Protecting Children Against Sexual Abuse,* Publication 1154, www.ocfs.state.ny.us./main/publications/Pub1154text.asp.

23. SafetyTat.com, *Found in the Crowd: Temporary Tattoos Keep Parents and Children Connected,* www.safetytat.com.

24. There are many sources that agree that 10-12 hours of sleep is the average needed, but the following article will help you gauge what your child's

individual needs are: Parenting and Child Health: Children, Youth, and Women's Health Service, *Sleep—3 Year to 5 Years,* www.cyh.com/HealthTopics/HealthTopicsDetails.aspx?p=114&np=122&id=1899.

25. Nemours Foundation, *Why Exercise is Wise,* www.kidshealth.org/teen/food_fitness/exercise/exercise_wise.html.

26. The recommendations were based on information taken from 34 school handbooks in 16 states in addition to my sources of registered nurses: Ruth Nau and Lindsey McConnell.

27. Health and Wellness Resource: Wyoming Valley Health Care System, *When to Keep Your Child Home from School,* www.wvhc.staywellsolutionsonline.com/library/Wellness/1,497.

28. Dr. Martha Simpson, Family Medicine, *Daughter Probably Has Infectious Pinkeye,* www.familymedicinenews.org.

29. Medicine Net.com, We Bring Doctors' Knowledge to You, *Strep Throat,* www.medicinenet.com/strep_throat/article.htm.

30. WebMD: Better information, Better health., Ear Infection Health Center, *Ear Infection—Symptoms,* www.webmd.com/cold-and-flu/ear-infection/ear-infection-symptoms.

31. WebMD: Better Information, Better Health., *Chickenpox (Varicella),* www.webmd.com/a-to-z-guides/chickenpox-varicella-topic-overview.

32. National Pediculosis Association, *Head Lice to Dead Lice,* www.headlice.org/.

33. CDC Website, Center for Disease Control: *Lice,* www.cdc.gov/ncidod/dpd/parasites/lice/factsht_head_lice.htm.

34. (National Pediculosis Assn.)

35. The Museum of Hoaxes, *Head-Lice Lotion Scam,* www.museumofhoaxes.com/hoax/weblog/comments/3811.

36. Hints and Things Website, *Treating Headlice,* www.hintsandthings.com/nursery/lice.htm.

37. (National Pediculosis Assn. Website.)

38. (CDC Website.)

39. (National Pediculosis Assn. Website.)

40. CFP-MFC Website: The Official Publication of Family Physicians of Canada, *Treating Children's Cyclic Vomiting,* www.pubmedcentral.nih.gov/articlerender.fcgi?artid=1949072.

41. Medi-Smart: Nursing Education Resources, *Treatment for Common Nosebleed,* www.medi-smart.com/fa-epistaxis.htm.

42. University of Michigan Health System, Pediatric Advisor 2006.2: *School Phobia,* www.med.umich.edu/1libr/pa/pa_bschphob_hhg.htm.

43. WebMD, *Sleep Disorders: The Buzz on Energy Drinks,* www.blogs.webmd.com/sleep-disorders/2007/08/buzz-on-energy-drinks.html.

44. American Heart Association, Learn and Live, *Fiber,* www.americanheart.org/presenter.jhtml?identifier=4574.

45. Child Health Alert Newsletter, September 1997, *Diet and Nutrition: Sorbitol and Diarrhea in Young Children,* www.childhealthalert.com/newsletters/sept97.htm.

46. .S. Department of Education, Archived Information, State of the Art Reading: November 1993, *Phonemic awareness, a precursor to competency in identifying words, is one of the best predictors of later success in reading.*

47. English Raven.com, *Dolch Sight-Word Resources for Reading,* www.englishraven.com/ttools_dolch.html.

48. Elaine McEwin-Akins, Educational Consultant, Parent Center Website, *Expert Answers: Is it normal that my preschooler wants to hear the same book over and over?* www.parentcenter.babycenter.com/404_is-it-normal-that-my-preschooler-wants-to-hear-the-same-book_69467.pc.

49. The College of Education, The University of Texas at Austin, Education Resources, *Talking Over Books: "Read it Again!",* www.edb.utexas.edu/resources/talking/.

50. Catherine Rauch, Parent Center Website, *Early Warning Signs of a Learning Disability,* www.parentcenter.babycenter.com/0_early-warning-signs-of-s-learning-disability_1382999.pc;jsessionid=36DD6296F46E195F47ABEB7C7844077B.01-03?print=true.

51. U.S. Department of Education, Office of Special Education Programs (OSEP's) IDEA Website, *Evaluation and Re-Evaluation,* www.idea.ed.gov/explore/view/p/%2Croot%2Cdynamic%2CqaCorner%2C3%2C

52. (U.S. Department of Education, *Evaluation and Re-Evaluation.)*

53. (U.S. Department of Education, *Evaluation and Re-Evaluation)*

54. Schools are required to provide parents with "procedural safeguards" so they will know exactly what their rights are in respect to special education services. In Ohio, the resource guide is entitled, *Whose IDEA is it anyway?*

The National Center for Learning Disabilities has also created a guide that is often used by schools to meet this federal regulation, entitled *IDEA Parent Guide,* which can be found at www.ncld.org/content/view/900/456084/.

55. (Wrightslaw.com, *No Child Left Behind.*)

56. United States Department of Health & Human Services, Office for Civil Rights, *Your Rights Under Section 504 of the Rehabilitation Act,* www.hhs.gov/ocr/504.html.

57. Harold Reasoner, *Cognitive Development in Elementary Students,* University of Texas: 2007, 28.

58. F.L. Clark, A.R. Mauck, J.A. McLoughlin, and J. Petrosko, J., "A Comparison of Parent-Child Perceptions of Student Learning Disabilities, *Journal of Learning Disabilities,* 1987, Vol. 20, No. 6, 357-360.

59. Great Schools, The Parents Guide to K12 Success, sponsored by Charles Schwab Learning, www.SchwabLearning.org.

60. Inspirational Quotes by Famous People with Learning Disabilities or Differences, www.lucarinfo.com/inspire/.

61. Wrights Law.com, A Memorandum from the United States Department of Education, written by Jeanette L. Lim, Acting Secretary for Civil Rights, Subject: *Clarification of School Districts' Responsibilities to Evaluate Children with Attention Deficit Disorders,* www.wrightslaw.com/info/add.eval.ocrmemo.htm.

62. Laura L. Bailet, PhD, Nemours Foundation: *Understanding Dyslexia,* August 2006, www.kidshealth.org/teen/diseases_condition/learning/dyslexia.html

63. U.S. Department of Education, *Title I Resources, Editor's Picks,* www.ed.gov/rschstat/eval/disadv/edpicks.jhtml.

64 Dr. Joseph M. Carver, Counseling Resource, *I Start Crying When I Have to Be Assertive,* www.counsellingresource.com/ask-the-psychologist/2008/06/03/crying-and-assertiveness/.

65. Free Health Encyclopedia: Healthy Living V1, *Benefits of Physical Activity and Exercise on the Body,* www.faqs.org/health/Healthy-Living-V1/Physical-Fitness.html.

66. L. Saunders, Ezine Articles, *Benefits of Martial Arts for Kids,* http://ezinearticles.com/?Benefits-of-Martial-Arts-Training-For-Kids&id=52697.

67. E.J. Sarma, Express It People, *Are You Skilled with Emotional Intelligence?* www.expressitpeople.com/20020318/management1.shtml.

68. U.S. Department of Education Website, a letter to parents regarding the disclosure of educational records to stepparents, from LeRoy Rooker, the Director of the Family Policy Compliance Office, www.ed.gov/policy/gen/guide/fpca/ferpa/library/hastings082004.html.

69. (U.S. Department of Education, FERPA.)